Dreaming With Your Eyes Wide Open

"Dream with open eyes and
make them come true."
T.E. Lawrence

Dr. Eleanor Newhouse Graves

PRESS

Dreaming With Your Eyes Wide Open
by Dr. Eleanor Newhouse Graves

Printed in the United States of America

ISBN 9781613796924

www.xulonpress.com

I dedicate this book to my first love,
Jesus Christ and the "love of my life,"
Michael

Acknowledgements

I am grateful for the editing assistance and encouragement received from Mrs. Lucille Seibert, Dr. Chris Jackson, Ms. Michaele Jacobs and Dr. Chestina Archibald.

I thank my family for their constant support. The skeleton outline for this book was written by my husband before his transition. Thanks, Michael.

I thank God for this "dream seed" that has taken on a "life of its own" and Jesus Christ for the promised dream of a heavenly home.

About the Dreamer

Bishop Michael Lee Graves, B.S., M.Div., D.Min.

The founding pastor of the Temple Church in Nashville, Tennessee was the consummate dreamer. He was always dreaming with his eyes wide open.

"Batavia, Illinois, a small town nestled in mid-America, USA, grew the eldest son of five children who would embrace the leadership role of his siblings when his mother became a single parent. He would continue his journey of faith to rise to leadership positions in his high school as student council president. Out of this small town, a young man would step foot on the campus of the American Baptist College and answer the biblical question posed in the times of Christ. Can any good thing come out of *Nazareth*?

If Batavia and ABC could be likened to *Nazareth,* then *YES* is the resounding response. Out of Batavia and out of ABC came Michael Lee Graves. Out of Michael Lee Graves came the presence and power of God.

Meanwhile, Marshall, Texas would already have given birth to a child who would grow into a young woman whose accomplishment propelled her into places of great significance. Her move from Marshall, Texas to her arrival in the leadership and political capital of the world, Washington, D.C., would become the stage for romance and marriage. However, it was not just the marriage of two people, but of two dreamers, two visionaries, two leaders, two spirits full of faith, and two hearts filled with hope, love and the expectation of excellence."

(From the video: "The life of a dreamer- Michael Lee Graves" – script written by Rev. Nelby Littleton)

The Temple Church in Nashville, Tennessee, was founded in August, 1977 with two members, Michael and Eleanor Graves. From that humble beginning, God has miraculously added to the church that now has over 4,000 members. The dream of a church where God is glorified, ministry matters and a positive spirit persists, has become a living, breathing organism called the Temple Church of Nashville.

Dr. Graves was a preacher par excellence. In his sermonic deliveries, the Word of God shook Nashville, awakened sleeping giants of idleness and apathy and challenged hypocrisy. This book is based on his sermons of help and hope. He inspired, encouraged and enabled many people to open their eyes to the possibilities of their own potential. He preached in many countries: from Korea and Sweden, to Israel, and South Africa. Wherever his message went, it was received with great enthusiasm and joy.

At the end of Dr. Graves' professional career training at the American Baptist Theological Seminary in Nashville, he graduated Summa Cum Laude and then proceeded to matriculate at the Wesley Theological Seminary in Washington, D.C.. While there, several of his professors who had taught Dr. Martin Luther King, Jr. recognized the potential of this young man.

Dr. Graves' call to the pastoral ministry brought him back to Nashville, Tennessee in July, 1970. After serving faithfully at the Pilgrim Emanuel Baptist Church from 1970 to 1977, he and his wife prayerfully resigned from that church to begin a new movement .This new movement revolutionized traditional approaches to ministry, with emphasis on the whole person, excellence in every aspect, a balance in worship styles and positive thinking.

Dr. Graves extended this influence as he served as the Director of Publications for the National Baptist Publishing Board. He served on various boards, and was appointed by Governor Lamar Alexander to the University of Tennessee Board of Regents. His leadership abilities were recognized nationally and locally as he taught ministers in the National Congress of the National Baptist Convention of America, Inc. He also was chosen to become a participant in Leadership Nashville. Another notable achievement was his election to the prestigious Morehouse School of Preachers at Morehouse College, Atlanta, Georgia.

Perhaps his crowning academic achievement was participating in the Oxford Round Table at St. Anthony's College at the University of Oxford, in Oxford, England on August 19, 2004, presenting the paper, "Scaling The Wall of Separation Between Church and State: Meeting the Educational Needs of Children and Youth".

Certainly, the highest honor of his life was his consecration as Bishop on August 3, 2004 in the apostolic line of succession of Peter. It was his dream comes true.

His life and legacy were a journey of dreams coming true until his sudden transition from earth to heaven on December 7, 2004. His death left many of his dreams unrealized, one of which was this work. He was producing the outline for this book at that time.

This book is lovingly dedicated to him.

About the author

Eleanor Newhouse Graves, B.S. M.Ed.

Eleanor, the widow of Bishop Graves, is a consultant, counselor, therapist, writer, college professor, diversity trainer, and motivational speaker. For over fifteen years, she taught ministers' wives on the national level.

Her undergraduate training began at George Washington University, in Washington, D.C., where she earned an undergraduate degree in zoology. Her studies then continued at the Antioch-Putney graduate school in Philadelphia, Pennsylvania. It was during this period of time that she met Michael Lee Graves at the Shiloh Baptist Church in Washington, D.C. They married in June, 1970 and began their lives together in Nashville, Tennessee in July of 1970. She completed her graduate degree in Guidance and Counseling with honors at Tennessee State University.

She has traveled extensively and her worldwide travels have provided a global perspective which continues to define her ministry in the United States, Canada, France, Africa and China.

She has served on several boards , including the Tennessee Repertory Theater, Operation Andrew and the Faith Family Medical Center. She was a participant in Leadership Nashville in 1983.Her ministry has widened having initiated the opening of the H.O.P.E. Wellness Center at the Temple Church focusing on the physical, spiritual, mental and financial health of persons. Serving as a model, there are now similar centers in New York, Connecticut, Kentucky and the Bahamas. There is now established a "Lady Graves Leadership Academy" affording young girls the tools to become Christian women in leadership positions. She has also been honored to host the "Eleanor Graves Christian Cotillion," an event designed to train young ladies to gracefully enter Christian society.

On May 15, 2010, Eleanor was granted the honorary degree of Doctor of Humane Letters from Faith Christian University and Schools. She is currently President and CEO of the Graves Foundation, an organization dedicated to improving the educational and health opportunities of underserved children and youth in the world's most challenging places.

As a helper to her husband, Eleanor has dreamed with her eyes wide open. Motivated and compelled to complete this book after her husband's transition, the publishing of this work is a DREAM COME TRUE.

Eleanor and Michael are the parents of Michael Lee Graves II, Ayanna Graves Moore, Ariel Williamson Newhouse Graves and Dana Guest. They have three grandchildren, Preston Eugene, Ravyn Alana and Michayla Leigh Moore.

Table of Contents

"All men dream, but not equally. Those who dream by night in the dusty recesses of their minds wake in the day to find out it was vanity; but the dreamers of the day are dangerous men, for they may act on their dream with open eyes, to make it possible. "

– T.E. Lawrence

Introduction

Daydreamers usually have great ideas but do nothing. They dream during the day, thus the word, *daydreaming*. I challenge you in this book to do more than daydream, but to dream with your eyes wide open and to do something with your dream!

God gives you dreams. Think about it. How many times have you had a wonderful idea, did nothing about it, then later discovered someone else did it? God, the creator, is the originator of dreams. He has given you a dream, maybe many dreams.

Everyone has a dream!

Your dream may be to finish a college degree, start a business, raise a family, become a millionaire, or make the world a better place. In this book, you will discover seven biblically-based, simple, and practical principles for taking an idea from your head and heart and transferring on to paper and then transforming to reality

Throughout this book, you will be invited to experience life stories of people who differ in ages, gender, racial and ethnic identity, social strata and geographical origin. But although diverse in nature, they possess a thread of similarity. All are shining examples of the seven principles outlined in this book. Yes, it is this common thread that unites them as superb teachers. **I am privileged to introduce them to you as you begin your own journey of "Dreaming With Your Eyes Wide Open"**

In **"Dreaming with Your Eyes Wide Open"**, you will discover the powerful principles of:

Perception
Purpose
Partnership
Possession
Perseverance
Positive Spirit
Power Beyond Yourself

I invite you to OPEN YOUR EYES! DREAM!

Dreams are the touchstones of our characters. For in dreams we but act a part which must have been learned and rehearsed in our waking hours. Our truest life is when we are in dreams awake.

HENRY DAVID THOREAU (1817–1862)

Perception: See the dream

Chapter One

What is your dream?

Shivering and huddled in the dense shrubbery, gazing up at the full moon with muscles and mind tired from the work of the day, William takes a pause. He has been running like a madman through the foggy air, obsessed and compelled by a dream. He has had this dream since he was a little boy:

> "I had a dream, a happy dream, I dreamed that I was free,
> And in my own bright land again there was a home for me,
> Savannah's tide rushed bravely on, I saw wave roll o'er wave,

And when in full delight I awoke, I found myself a slave."

(The Slaves' Dream – written by
William C. Caroll)

In the distance, he hears the barking of hound dogs; he is jolted to reality and starts running again. It is now or he will never be free. He sees a little woman running ahead of him ,the same little woman who whispered in his ear and planted in his brain an image of freedom not so long ago.

She, too, beaten and abused, had the same dream as a little girl. Her injuries had been so severe that she would sometimes instantaneously just fall asleep without any prior notice. But tonight she does not sleep. Her eyes are wide open as she and William move steadily and carefully along the secret route so familiar to her. Together they run and run through Maryland, then Philadelphia and finally to Canada ... to **FREEDOM**. William is free! His childhood dream has become reality!

From some other existence, the little woman smiles, for in some mysterious way, she shares the dream. The woman leading him to freedom is named Araminta. At five years old, Araminta was "rented" to neighbors to do housework. She was never very good at household chores and was beaten regularly by her owners and those who "rented" her. She was, of course, not educated to read or write. She eventually was assigned work as a field hand, which she preferred to household work. Although she was a small woman, she was strong, her time working in the fields probably contributing to her strength.

At age fifteen, she sustained a head injury, when she deliberately blocked the path of the overseer pursuing an uncooperative fellow slave. In doing so, she herself was hit by the heavy weight the overseer sent hurling through the air at the other slave. Araminta, better known as Harriet, sustained a severe concussion. She was ill for a long time following this injury, and never fully recovered. She had periodic "sleeping fits" which, in the early years after her injury, made her less attractive as a slave to others who may have wanted her services. Harriet Tubman was only about five feet tall, but she was smart and she was strong — and she carried a long rifle.

This little lady speaks to us today as she did to William generations ago:

"Every great dream begins with a dreamer. Always remember, you have within you the strength, the patience, and the passion to reach for the stars to change the world."

Harriet Tubman

You are that dreamer! What is your dream?

In the introduction, you were challenged to think about the fact that you have at least one dream. It has come to you, maybe long ago or recently. What was it? Was it an idea for your health, wealth, family, personality, a better or different career, a better job, an exotic vacation, a dream home, an invention or perhaps improving society?

You have had these thoughts. I call them **"dream seeds". God "plants" these ideas in our minds. God's ideas are always good ideas.**

Everything in our world began as a thought. . God began the world as a thought. The first light bulb was first conceived as a thought. The first airplane began as a thought. Thinking has creative power.

*The first principle in dreaming with your eyes wide open is **PERCEPTION**.*

Perception: to take notice of, observe, detect and become aware of a thought in your mind. It also means that you achieve an understanding of it. You "see" it and then give it attention.

Perception is the lens through which you view life based on many factors, such as upbringing, beliefs, background, personality, racial identity, gender and age.

Perception enables you to recognize that you have a dream.

You must believe you can dream **"with your eyes wide open."** Believing heightens perception. You are not a 'daydreamer' who, with glazed over eyes, sits idly and stares into the sky. Instead, you are sitting at attention, getting ready to move toward what you "see".

You receive so many images every day with your **physical eyes that** you don't really notice. For example, there is an arrow in the FedEx sign. Have you seen it? Take a look the next time you see a FedEx truck. It is hidden in the EX of the sign. When our awareness is heightened, we have an "AH HA" moment.

You have had ideas float through your mind this week that escaped your attention. You didn't **perceive** them. You didn't capture the idea and consider it a reasonable thought. Sometimes these ideas come by chance in a fleeting moment. For example, the scientist, Arthur Fry, was at church. He sang in the choir and needed to quickly locate the different songs in the hymnal. He remembered that he had been working on a 'low-tack' adhesive developed by a colleague at the 3M Company. Somehow the company for years could not think of a way to use this adhesive developed in 1974. It was not marketable. In a split moment, Arthur Fry came up with an idea that impacts all of us now: **the Post-it note**. This product is now sold in more than 100 countries. Where would we be without it? He "saw" something others did not. He had heightened awareness.

Perception gives you the ability to see not only the visible, but also the invisible with your spiritual eyes. We do not live in a one-dimensional world, but one of many dimensions. There is another dimension that is spiritual .Once in a while, we get a glimpse into this spiritual realm and something illuminating and powerful happens.

There is such an account in the Bible (2 Kings 6:17). Elisha is with his servant and they are surrounded by the enemy. When the servant arises early in the morning and goes outside of his tent, he sees the enemies' chariots, perhaps even their spears, swords and knives glistening in the rising sun. He comes back frightened. Elisha says to the servant: "Don't worry about it because there are more with us than are with them." He saw the invisible army of God through the spiritual eyes of faith. **That's perception.**

You must come to the place where you can **perceive**, with God's help, the invisible. If you are having difficulty, pray and ask God to open your eyes in the same way Elisha did for his fearful servant.

Jesus spoke in parables or stories to help people see what they otherwise could not see. The disciples came up and asked, "Why do you tell stories?" He replied, "You've been given insight into God's kingdom. You know how it works. Not everybody has this gift, this insight; it hasn't been given to them. Whenever someone has a ready heart for this, the insights and understandings flow freely. But if there is no readiness, any trace of receptivity soon disappears. That's why I tell stories: to create readiness, to nudge the people toward receptive insight. In their present state they can stare till doomsday and not see it, listen till they're blue in the face and not get it."

"But you have God-blessed eyes—eyes that see! And God-blessed ears—ears that hear! A lot of people, prophets and humble believers among them, would have given anything to see what you are seeing, to hear what you are hearing, but never had the chance."

Matthew 10:13 (MSG)

Think about that! **You** have God-blessed eyes – eyes that see. It takes a ready heart for insight and understanding. Jesus calls it **receptive insight**. This is perception. Open your mind to the limitless possibilities. Many times these possibilities are right in front of you!

One such example is Hagar in the Old Testament book of Genesis. (Genesis 21) Hagar's dreams of a stable home and a future for her son were dashed when Abraham sent her away to the desert of Beersheba with a little food and water.

She was now homeless. She was wandering – hot, depressed, hungry, thirsty, helpless and hopeless .She needed water for survival. When the water provided by Abraham was depleted, she left her son, Ishmael, her hope of a future, under a shrub and went away. She said, "I can't watch my son die." As she sat, she broke into sobs.

The angel of God saw her predicament after hearing the boy cry. He asked, "What's wrong, Hagar? Don't be afraid. God has heard the boy and knows the fix he's in. "

Just then God **opened her eyes**. She looked .She saw a well of water. The very thing she needed was right there before her .Supplied with this immediate need, she was able to hear and understand another message from the angel representing God. This angel told her to get up, get going and that her son would be all that she hoped and dreamed of. God would make of him a great nation. With this head and heart "**dream seed**", she got up from her depressed state and headed for their future. Her ability to "see" what was originally hidden saved her life and that of her son. **Hagar saw the well that was always there. Regardless of your situation, God can open your eyes as he did Hagar's to new possibilities, to fresh springs of water in a desert land. You, too, can dream in the 'desert.'**

Perception means that we see situations right in front of us with new insight, wisdom and understanding.

> The voyage of discovery is not in seeking new landscapes but in having new eyes.
>
> MARCEL PROUST, "The Captive,"
> *Remembrance of Things Past*

Perception gives you the power to see dreams.

Jewell was a secretary on a university campus for twenty-six years. She was forty years old, divorced from her husband of twenty-five years, a victim of sexual abuse, with two children. There were people in her life who put her down, calling her "fat, old and stupid." She said, "I never thought I could be anything but a secretary, and I was good at that!" Needless to say, her self-esteem was at an all-time low. Her only hope was to work for another four years toward retirement.

A year later, while taking a class on "Experiencing God", and after an appendectomy, she began to open her eyes to the possibilities around her. Her problems, like Hagar's, were immense. Remember, she was now sick, divorced, with one daughter in college, her house in foreclosure, and with very little money. Her take- home paycheck was thirty-two dollars. From this meager income, she continued to tithe. The picture was not pretty. Her problems seemed to outweigh her possibilities.

During this time, she continued her Bible study and God spoke to her. He told her that He was going to take all the experiences of her life and He was going to use them to His glory. She relates, "I was going to be able to free women who had been sexually abused as children, who had been physically abused in their marriages, who had been raped – all the uncomfortable things women don't talk about in their church or among their friends." A "dream seed" was planted.

Jewell continued to work and after her divorce, experienced a longing. She couldn't figure it out. So, she started taking classes .Her daughter had graduated from college by this time and encouraged her mother to continue to work on the degree she had always wanted.

One day when Jewell's supervisor stood in front of her desk and said, "Well, it's nice for people to want dreams and education, but nobody in this office is going to be able to take day classes because it sets a bad precedent."

It was on that day she sought the Lord .She didn't want her dream to die.

God sparked something in her spirit. She thought, "I was on the campus all the time, in an educational environment. I can take classes." The well was there all the time. She now saw what she needed and her "dream seed" took root. She resigned her job and completed her under-graduate degree .But she didn't stop there. She continued her education at the University of Illinois and is now Dr. Jewell, Ph.D.

Perception gives you the power to see the possibilities instead of the problems. It opens your eyes to opportunities you might have missed right in front of you.

Lack of perception can lead to a dull life of mediocrity.

DO NOT BE CONTENT LIVING YOUR LIFE IN A RUT.

Consider this: We sometimes go through life "on automatic."

WAKE UP AND DREAM

It all goes by in the blink of an eye
From one "get it done" to another
More and more tasks I cram into each day
Putting myself last after all the others.

I don't know how it came to this
As a child I had many dreams
Life snuck up and I lost myself
Or at least that's how it seems.

I long each night for sleep to come
For when I close my eyes, I am free
No more lists to check things off
While I dream, I am free to be ME

I come alive as I fall asleep
And dream of living true
I dream of the place I long to see
And all that I yearn to do

If only I could **dream with my eyes wide
open**
I wonder how life would be
If only I could believe again
And awaken the Dreamer in me

The time has come to wake up my Dreamer
And get clear on what I desire
To believe in myself, make my life better
And become the very Dreamer I admire

It's your time to WAKE UP and DREAM

Poem by Kelly Moore
Certified dream coach

Without perception, it's the same old thing,
the same old way, the same old thinking- the

same things all the time. We listen to the same music, drive home the same way every day. We experience nothing new or nothing fresh. We need to get out of a rut and think new thoughts. Your idea may be just the thought needed to change a generation, cure cancer, improve your financial status, and advance the kingdom of God. Remember, these "dream seeds" come from God.

God's ideas are good ideas.

"We must nurture our dreams like we would a child. They are **God-given** and just as precious. Without ambitions how would a child learn to ride a bicycle, play an instrument or whistle? We deny the spirit of God when we as adults settle for less than our dreams!"

Conway Stone

Chapter One Summary

Everyone has a dream or many dreams.

These are ideas and thoughts that come from God. They are "dream seeds."

Perception gives you the power to see these dreams. It opens your eyes.

Perception helps you to see the invisible, improbable, and seemingly impossible.

God's ideas are good ideas.

Points to Ponder

"Go confidently in the direction of your dreams. Live the life you have imagined."

Henry David Thoreau

"We lift ourselves by our thought. We climb upon our vision of ourselves. If you want to enlarge your life, you must first enlarge your thought of it and of yourself. Hold the ideal of yourself as you long to be, always everywhere."

Orison Swett Marden

What life do you imagine? How do you want your life to be?

Take time to sit quietly and ask God to open your spiritual eyes.

Write down what He reveals to you. These ideas may not come all at one time. You may need inspiration from a book, nature, an inspiring movie, traveling to a new place or just being still. Some ideas may actually come while you are asleep. Keep a pad or recording device near your bed to capture these dreams.

Chapter Two

Perception gives you a unique look at life.

A lady was traveling during the holiday period and in her traveling she became quite frustrated with delayed flights, lost luggage, overcrowded spaces and overbooked flights. And so, in the lull of waiting for her next flight, she bought a newspaper. At an overcrowded restaurant she found one little table that had two chairs, bought herself some coffee, a little bag of cookies and sat down to have herself a quiet time to read her newspaper, eat her cookies and drink her coffee.

In that crowded little restaurant, a well-dressed little boy came and sat across from her. She put down her paper and looked at him. Immediately she re- opened her paper and thought," the nerve of that little boy to sit down at my table without my permission!" As she is sitting there sipping on her coffee and reading her newspaper, she hears the rattling of paper and she notices that the little boy has her bag of cookies and he is beginning to eat them. She doesn't know what to say to the little boy. She doesn't want to be cold and cruel, so she simply slides her hand under the newspaper, reaches into the bag of cookies and eats one.

To her consternation, he continues to eat her cookies, getting yet another cookie. They go back and forth until there is only one cookie left. The little boy takes the cookie, breaks it in half, and slides it under the newspaper so that she can at least have the last half of "her" cookie. About this time, she hears her flight called. She folds her newspaper, gulps down the rest of her coffee and picks up her bag. She looks in her purse to get her ticket.

Behold! There is her bag of cookies. She has been eating **the little boy's cookies**. She was certain that the cookies she was eating belonged to her. Her perspective, her perception was all wrong. Many of us go through life with that kind of warped perception.

"When you're in the muck you can only see muck. If you somehow manage to float above it, you still see the muck but you see it from a different perspective. And you see other things too." – David Cronenberg

Think about this: Have you ever gone to the eye doctor to get new glasses? You really were able to see. You perhaps drove yourself there. You didn't run into anybody in your car. You noticed the great big signs. You made it safely there to get your eyes checked. When you waited around for an hour and your glasses were ready, you put them on. Wow! You began to see things so much better. There were some things you really never saw until you got your new glasses. Your warped and distorted vision was corrected.

A young couple moves into a new neighborhood. The next morning while they are eating breakfast, the young woman sees her neighbor hanging the wash outside. "That laundry is not very clean", she said. "She doesn't know how to wash correctly. Perhaps she needs better laundry soap." Her husband looked on, but remained silent. Every time her neighbor would hang her wash to dry, the young woman would make the same comments. About one month later, the woman was surprised to see a nice clean wash on the line and said to her husband: "Look, she has learned how to wash correctly. I wonder who taught her this." The husband said, "I got up early this morning and cleaned our windows."

When you look at **the world situation**, your vision can become warped and distorted. When you look at the present economy, you may see a dismal picture. Your view from your "side of the world" can affect your perception of what is possible.

You see what you expect to see and society can be the filter of these expectations. What you see is often colored by other factors such as your personality type, your gender, or your self-esteem, your personal beliefs, your emotional state, your social experiences, your cognitive maturity, and your spiritual maturity.

Our perceptions can be biased by our **own low self-esteem and fear.** These place a greater attention on ourselves and on the risk of having dreams that cause others to think we are 'crazy', unrealistic, and foolish. When we take on such a perspective, our perception is hampered and our ability to dream is lessened. We can be affected by our **personal belief system and concepts** which construct the boundaries between what is real and unreal, what is achievable and unachievable, what is possible and impossible.

Our expectations were thoroughly 'unwarped' when Barack Obama became President of the United States. So many people said they thought they would never see an African American elected President of the United States in their lifetime. It seemed, according to society, to be an impossible dream. Obviously, President Obama was not guilty of this thinking. His dream was not constricted by what society expected.

- Christopher Columbus dreamed of a world that was round contrary to popular belief. He looked beyond the physical and the known geographical horizon. People thought he was crazy!
- The Wright brothers believed that man could fly with the help of a machine called an airplane. Their horizon to overcome was the pull of gravity that restricted upward movement into the air. People thought they were crazy!

When you look at your horizon, what do you see? Horizon is defined as the limitation of one's ability to perceive. Can you look past the horizon and see the possibilities?

People thought that my husband was crazy! In our first pastorate, after seven successful years, the church situation looked ideal. The debt on the new church had just been removed. The worship services were bustling, with new members joining every Sunday. People were being turned away for lack of space. There was a need to build a larger facility with room for community activities. The lay leadership said: "Pastor, all you have to do is come and preach each Sunday."

This was not Pastor's dream. His dream was to be involved in a ministry that was meaningful – one that would address the issues of educating children, feeding and clothing the homeless. As a young, idealistic couple, we envisioned and expected a church where people loved each other and loved the people in the community. The Pastor and the church leaders looked at the same situation, but with different perspectives. Pastor Graves saw possibilities, the leaders saw problems.

You cannot allow your ability to perceive your dreams to be restricted in any way. Move past the limits of your horizon.

"Perspective, as its inventor remarked, is a beautiful thing. What horrors of damp huts, where human being languish, may not become picturesque through aerial distance! What hymning of cancerous vices may we not languish over as sublimest art in the safe

remoteness of a strange language and artificial phrase!"　　　　　**George Eliot**

Do you know who George Eliot was?

George Eliot, better known as Mary Ann Evans, certainly had a unique perspective on life. She was a single, working woman in the male-dominated 1800's. She was a writer with a male pen name. Her name allowed her to write something other than cookbooks and the traditional female genre of writing. She dared to dream that she could write freely as a man would write during those times. Mary Ann Evans was one of the greatest writers in English literature. She did not allow her gender or society to prevent her from her dream of becoming a writer.

When you look at your dream, does it seem crazy? It may seem so, but don't allow that to deter you. Hold on, as we go on to the next chapter.

Chapter Two Summary

Perception gives you a unique way of looking at things.

Don't be afraid of ideas that may seem crazy or unrealistic.

Perspective is determined by many factors, both positive and negative. Don't allow a "warped" perspective to cloud your perception and ability to dream. Dare to move past your horizon (the limitation of your ability to perceive) and dream of the impossible.

Points to ponder

"Don't be afraid of the space between your dreams and reality. If you can dream it, you can make it so."   Belva Davis

What warped ideas block your thinking and close your mind to your dreams? Here are a few:

- Only visionaries have dreams
- Only young people have dreams
- Only old people have dreams
- I don't have time to dream
- I am trying to survive
- I don't have money for a dream
- I am afraid I will fail
- I am afraid I will succeed
- I don't have enough education
- I am too fat, ugly, stupid
- This is a man's world
- That's crazy!

Chapter Three

Perception can project you into the future.

Have you ever experienced computer imaging?

If you go to a plastic surgeon, he can show you by computer how you will look after a face-lift or a tummy tuck. If you go to a police department looking for a missing child, they can show you how that child, who was abducted five years ago, would look today .If you went to an upscale beauty salon, the hair stylist could show you how you would look with blonde hair or short hair. **Computer imaging.**

Your brain is greater than any computer. You can imagine and perceive how your life would be if you live out your dreams .**Perception can project you into the future.**

What is your ideal life?

What would you be doing? Who would you be?

Where would you live? How would you live?

What kind of family life would you have?

What significant accomplishment would you achieve?

It's sort of like working on a puzzle. You must pick up a potential piece and look at it and then imagine whether it fits the empty space even before you place it.

It is also like reading a mystery novel. Whether right or wrong, you can think about the outcome and "who did it". Your mind can easily float from the present to the future.

Remember that God has planted the "dream seed." Once you are firmly aware of this "dream seed", you can visualize yourself living this dream.

If you want a new house, you can walk in it before it is on the architect's drawing board. That is the power of perception.

If you are dreaming of a college education, you must first see yourself walking across the front of the auditorium in your cap and gown, raising your hand to receive that wonderful piece of paper.

World situations change because of visionary world leaders who see a better world. Robert Kennedy, paraphrasing George Bernard Shaw, said, "Some people see things as they are and ask why – I see things as they can be and ask, why not?"

The world leader against apartheid in South Africa, Archbishop Desmond Tutu, challenges us with these words:

"It is saying that the world cares about oppression and injustice, and it is saying to our people that this is their prize — don't give up. Don't give up the struggle. There is a light at the end of the Tunnel.

Today I behold the world through the eyes of Spirit. I look beyond appearances to find a glimmer of beauty, an element of positivity or a spark of the divine potential in everyone and everything. As I observe, I see things as they can be, not as they appear. In this way, I am a visionary for God and for Good. Amen. Amen. Amen."

The process of conjuring up a strong mental image of what we want in our mind is called **creative visualization.** Whatever you conceive and believe, with God, you can achieve. It is essential in dreaming with your eyes wide open.

When you hold in your mind a dream, even 'seeing' yourself doing it, and living it, you are actually creating new neural pathways in your brain. The brain is a wonderful and mysterious organ. By visualizing, your brain sees this image as so. It does not immediately distinguish between what you visualize and what you are actually experiencing. The subconscious and conscious are coexistent. You subsequently interpret what you see by what you believe. **Perception controls our reality.**

Have you ever thought about buying a new car? It seems as though you see that car just about everywhere you go! That doesn't make it your car, but your consciousness level is heightened by the thought in your brain.

Visualization moves your dream from the subconscious to the conscious level. Once on this level, you can proceed to making this dream become reality.

So, how do you do this?

Art Stanley gives ways to visualize. He says we must" first relax and unwind. Get quiet and clear your mind of the mental chatter that most of us experience throughout the typical day. Stop the barrage of thoughts and you stop the resistance. Ultimately you're striving to reach a state of peace and tranquility. It's what Wayne Dyer refers to as 'the space between your thoughts.' … Once you've reached your state of ultimate relaxation…that's when you begin to build a mental picture…Make it something you really desire. ..As you visualize in greater detail, your image begins to take shape, dimension and color as it comes to vibrant life…Expand on your description and create a vivid picture of it in your mind. Feel that it's yours already and really crank up those feelings. As your desire gains intensity and strength, it propels you forward to your dream."

He continues to say, "Visualization puts almost anything within your reach."

Source: Art Stanley (http://www.law-of-abundance-living.com/create-the-life-you-want.html)

Napoleon Hill said it best in *Think and Grow Rich* when he said, "Whatever the mind of man can conceive and believe it can achieve."

Creative visualization is the act of conceiving your dream. It is actually listening to the voice of God as He is planting your "dream seed." It connects your mind with the mind of God, who gives us the dream. It produces an extraordinary energy, enthusiasm and passion that propel you forward. It can begin the process of dream realization. You will begin to recognize that you and God are co-creators.

Chapter Summary

Perception can project you into the future. Creative visualization is conjuring a strong, detailed image of your dream in your mind.

It is essential in the process of making your dreams come true.

You realize that you and God are co-creators in this process.

As you visualize, you gain energy, enthusiasm and passion for your dream, propelling you toward action.

Points to ponder

Picture the dream that you would most like to create using the steps outlined above. You can use your imagination to reinforce the image you have in mind and if any negative thoughts arise when you are visualizing, then simply let the negative thoughts go!

You can also visualize all the steps involved in reaching your dream and not just the outcome. To do this, simply start out with your final step in mind and then work your way backwards until you reach the first step or where you are now. Write your thoughts down immediately. Take your time to listen to God.

Principle Two

Purpose: Realize Why You Have a Dream

"We are born purpose-seeking creatures. Purpose is necessary for our very health and survival. If you doubt this, check out the rates of illness and death when people lose or give up their sense of purpose."

Richard Leider

Chapter Four

Why do I have a dream?

We now have a dream in mind and are ready to act. There is a missing link! Why do we have a dream? Why does God give us a dream?

The basketball star, Charles Barkley says that there are two important days: the day you were born and the day you discover why you were born.

Why were you born? What are you doing here on earth?

What are you living for? The way you live and how you spend your time is an indicator of your reason for living.

Is it to make money?
-have fun
-get smart
-work hard
-love people
-have a nice house, car
-go on an exotic vacation

Face the truth!

Do you truly enjoy your life?
How do you look for satisfaction and fulfillment?
How do you spend your day?

You are not meant to just exist and live a dull day-to-day, 9 to 5 existence. Most people are so busy surviving, working at a job just for the money and living for the weekend that they are happy just to be getting through the day.

Headline: 'Sense of Purpose' Keeps Her Going – Dorothy Height Celebrates 97th Birthday in D.C.
JET magazine, June 21, 2009

Dorothy Height, who had just turned 97, making her the oldest active civil rights leader, says, "I always had a sense of purpose and that drives you and keeps you moving." She was the chairwoman emeriti of the National Council of Negro Woman, headquartered in Washington, D.C.

The magazine continues, "When it comes to her legacy, she says, 'I want the world to remember that I had a commitment to social justice and I tried to achieve it. My legacy is more that I have stayed by my purpose from my youth to today, and I am 97.'"

Dorothy Height died April 20, 2010. What a wonderful and unique woman!

When you take time to discover and define your purpose, your life and your dreams will energize you and motivate you to act and begin living a life, as did Dr. Height, on purpose.

What is the meaning of the word, purpose? The word comes from Old French, *porpos,* meaning "aim, intention".

Your purpose is who you are and what gets you excited. Your purpose is why you are here. You were born for a purpose. God has a plan for your life.

I was talking with my grandchildren, Preston, Ravyn and Michayla, describing the gist of this book. I introduced to them the word, *purpose.*

In my attempt to simplify the concept for these three, all under the age of nine years, I explained that purpose is the reason God placed you here on earth. I went on the say that your "highest" purpose is to honor God, to make God proud of you. Immediately, their "simple", yet profound question became, "What is my purpose?" Of course, this is an ongoing conversation!

What do the scriptures say?

> "It's in Christ that we find out who we are and what we are living for. Long before we first heard of Christ...he had his eye on us, had designs on us for glorious living, part of the overall **purpose** he is working out in everything and everyone."
>
> Ephesians 1:11 (MSG)

You find your purpose in Christ. He has a design and a dream for you.

Finding purpose gives life meaning.

Rick Warren states, "Without purpose, life is motion without meaning, activity without direction, and events without reason. Without God, life has no purpose, and without purpose, life has no meaning. Without meaning, life has no significance or hope."

I was inspired by an article on the life of Ken Goslin. ("A Life Resurrected", by Bob Smietana The TENNESSEAN, April 24, 2011)

Ken is a homeless man, born in San Francisco. He has spent most of his life, including his childhood, as a homeless person. He was moved from one foster home to another. At the age of 7, he encountered an abusive family in

Georgia that taught him to trust no one and to believe that no one really cared for him.

This experience propelled him to live on the streets at the age of 14. He worked at times, with no stable job. His life was filled with "booze and drugs." He moved from Atlanta to Nashville in 2010. His health began to deteriorate and he was diagnosed with a growing brain tumor that could give him only six months to live. This tumor also destroyed his ability to speak and walk. He uses a pen and notepad to communicate.

Goslin was befriended by a woman in Atlanta who works with homeless people. This encounter, along with meeting two other friends, a Nashville nurse and a Vanderbilt Divinity student, helped to develop in him a sense of family and community. He now realizes that God cares about him. He has become a "believer". He said that, because of his faith, he's not afraid anymore. He related at a vespers service his feeling that, for the first time, God loved him.

"I believe I am here for a reason." What a powerful statement to make before one dies! Lauren Jones, the influential nurse from Guardian Hospice said that Goslin has taught her how to be brave despite circumstances. She said, "The way he finds a way to laugh at whatever circumstances – that has taught me what joy is." Goslin's sense of humor often keeps his visitors laughing even after they leave.

I can only surmise that Ken Goslin's dream was to have a family and someone who cared about him. After a lifetime of negative experiences and now health challenges, he has finally realized his dream through the love and care of several of God's "angels." He has found a purpose for his life. He has also found hope for his future. He said when he dies, "I know where I am going."

I believe that Ken Goslin had a dream. I also believe that you have a dream.

In the January 2011 issue of The *Contributor,* a newspaper written and distributed by homeless people, there is this moving poem by Chris Scott, a formerly homeless songwriter (chrisfie-selman@aol.com).

Dream Wings

Life spent with no accomplishment's
not really life at all
Afraid to fly… So you never try…Never
have to fall…
You were meant for bigger things than a
cage of security
Take a chance… Spread your wings…
Learn what it means to be free

*Let your dreams be your wings…Carry you
to better things…*
Be courageous and be strong
When the whole world says you're wrong
*Take to flight…Know you're right…What
you do…*
*And let your dreams be the wings
that carry you…*

Don't be bound feet on the ground…Destined
for a whole lot more…
The answers will be found where none have
gone before
Make the most of the life you live… Don't
settle for anything less…
Show the world what you've got to give…Be
better than all the rest…

Let your dreams be your wings...Carry you to
better things...
Be courageous and be strong
When the whole world says you're wrong
Take to flight...Know you're right...What
you do...
And let your dreams be the wings
that carry you...

Believe it will come to be...Persevere past
others' point of view...
Rise above mere mediocrity...Reach new
heights and see it through...
An ocean of excuses... A thousand
reasons why...
Let go of them and be one who chooses
To spread your wings and fly...

Let your dreams be your wings...Carry you to
better things...
Be courageous and be strong
When the whole world says you're wrong
Take to flight... Know you're right...What
you do...
And let your dreams be the wings
that carry you...

Why do you have a dream?

Your purpose is directly related to your dreams. Your purpose defines why you are here and your dreams are an expression of your purpose. Living out your dreams means that you are fulfilling your purpose in life.

Let's take a moment to examine what purpose is NOT:

1. Reaching goals and being successful is not the same as fulfilling your life's purpose. There are many successful people who are not living out their purpose.
2. Working at a job is not necessarily the same as fulfilling your life's purpose. It may be just a way of surviving.
3. You won't discover life's meaning by just looking within yourself. You must start with focus on God and his plan for your life.

"You were made by God and for God – and until you understand that life will never make sense."

"Life is about letting God use you for His purposes, not you using Him for your own purposes."

Rick Warren, *The Purpose Driven Life*

So, how do you discover your purpose?

To discover your purpose, you must answer these questions:
Who am I?
Where am I?
Where am I going?
What am I doing?

These are not easy questions to answer. I challenge you to keep reading as we uncover perhaps uncharted territory in the following chapters.

Chapter Five

Who Am I?

Take a good look at yourself in the mirror. Who are you?

Take a long look at your life and the choices you have made. Are you living according to your purpose or are you just going through the motions?

Dr. Brad Swift, in his book, *Life On Purpose: Six Passages to An Inspired Life*, states that the way we accomplish our purpose should be powerful (in shaping our lives), enduring (lasting beyond our lifetime) and flexible (room to play and express ourselves – through the seasons of our lives.)

Our purpose is shaped by the following elements:

Vision: What is the vision or possibility you see for the world?

Values: What are the core values you stand for and are willing to give your life for?

Being: Who are you? What can people count on from you? Life purpose is more about who you are than what you do.

The fourth component, according to Swift, is the foundation and glue that holds it all together - **Love**! Swift says, "When we combine this glue with your unique vision of what's possible in the world, your unique set of values, and your unique qualities of being, we end up with a powerful, empowering, and enduring life purpose that still has ample room for us to play and express ourselves. This life purpose becomes the context that shapes and forms us as we go about doing all the things that make up our life."

So, who are you?

"When you have a sense of your own identity and a vision of where you want to go in your life, you then have the basis for reaching out to the world and going after your dreams for a better life."   Stedman Graham

People who don't know who they are fall below their privilege.

Let's see who you are according to scripture:

Psalm 139 says that you are important to God. It says that you are "fearfully and wonderfully made". You are one of a kind.

We can say more:

1. **You are God's child**. He made you, loves you deeply and cares for you.

   "Because of his love, God had already decided that through Jesus Christ he would make us his children – that was his pleasure and purpose." Ephesians 1:5

2. **You were custom designed by God with specific talents, gifts, skills and abilities.**

   I Peter 4:10-11, 2Cor. 8:19
   "God works through different men in different ways, but it is the same God who achieves his purposes through them all." I Cor. 12:6

3. You were meant to be happy and content by living within the plans God has for you. Those plans fit your purpose.

"The Lord has made everything for his own purposes .If you are not living and dreaming within the plans God has for you, you will be unhappy and restless." Prov. 16:4

Points to ponder

Answer these questions: Take your time to discover who you are.

1. What is the vision or possibility you see for the world?

2. What are the core values you stand for and are willing to give your life for?

3. Who are you? What can people count on from you?

4. What are your unique gifts and abilities? (Take a spiritual gifts inventory. Many are available online.)

More questions:
What do you really enjoy? What excites you? What would you do even if you weren't paid to do it? What do you do and suddenly realize that time has gone by?

Michael Jordan, one of the greatest basketball players of all time said:

> "Some people want it to happen and some wish it to happen, but others make it happen. I truly love the game; I wouldn't be playing if I didn't love the game. I'm not getting paid astronomical dollars; it's truly for the love of the game of basketball."

Pierre Omidyar, who became a billionaire through the Internet with successful companies like eBay, says, "I was just pursuing what I enjoyed doing. I mean, I was pursuing my passion. I've got a passion for solving a problem that I can solve in a new way. And that maybe it helps that nobody has done it before as well."

What makes the difference between those wanting, wishing and making it happen? What makes the difference between a dreamer of the night and a "dreamer of the day?"

One word: ACTION

Perception plus positive emotion (passion) equals action.

You've got to get moving!!

~ Vision without action is a daydream. Action without vision is a nightmare.

Japanese proverb

"I felt like I wasn't really living, and there was nothing compelling about the path I was on. I realized I'd have to take charge"

Shelby Monroe

Shelby Monroe graduated from college with a degree in English Literature – and no idea what to do next. So she did a bit of everything. She taught college classes, worked in a bookstore, opened her own bookstore. After going to library school, which she found boring, she made the statement above.

She was now 40 years old. A friend who was deployed in Iraq casually suggested that she become an embedded reporter.

"It took just a few days, maybe less, for me to start thinking seriously about the idea," she says. She got started. However, the Department of Defense was not accepting any new reporters. She persevered and began her dream job.

She says, "It takes a certain amount of bravery to do something you never expected to do, especially having no example to follow." She decided to act. Remember Jewell?

She was divorced, forty years old, with no money, and two children. She had a dream of an education beyond what she presently had. After her supervisor's remark regarding her not being able to take day classes, she made a decision that day. She knew that she could not get full retirement benefits because she needed thirty years of service, not twenty-eight.

"But the Lord said move, and I did. Scared to death, but I moved. I wrote my letter of resignation. I went back to the classroom." She decided to act.

Another instance was that Sunday in July, 1977. It was hot and humid. It was comfortable, however in the sanctuary as Pastor Graves began his sermon. He preached with power and the people responded, as usual, in the call/response tradition of the Black Baptist church. "Preach, Rev.", "Tell the truth! " "Amen" At the end of the sermon, after the customary invitation to the congregants to become a disciple of Jesus Christ, my husband told those listening that he had something to say.

Remember the dream? To serve the community with ministry that matters. That dream was slowly slipping away. What happened?

There was a lot of success in that first church. Children and new faces were "taking over" the church. A day care facility was established. The first bus ministry conducted by a Black church began to canvas the neighborhood and bring those persons, some unlike the congregants, to the church. The building was being used every day of the week – that was the dream beginning to come true. During this period of time, there were many accomplishments. The membership had grown so much that the newly built sanctuary could no longer hold the more than 1,000 worshippers trying to crowd in on Sunday. My husband would stand in dismay, looking out of his study window as people were turned away for lack of room. Something needed to be done. We would have to begin to build again to accommodate more people and expand to include new and innovative ministries to serve the community.

There were many who had just experienced the pain and agony of a building program. The new sanctuary was less than two years old. "Pastor, we only need you to preach on Sunday. You don't have to do any more than that. We don't want or need to build a larger space." Opposition arose and obstacles appeared. My husband was unhappy. He was so unhappy that our four-year-old daughter, Ayanna, noticed. She commented to him one day, "Poppa, why are you so sad?"

He was slow to respond. She said, "Is it because the people at church won't let you do what you want to do?" Out of the mouth of babes! "YES!" he had to admit.

My husband and I went on a retreat to the mountains of Tennessee. We prayed and decided to pursue the dream that obviously would not flourish in this church.

Let's return to that hot and humid Sunday in July. Pastor Graves had something to say as the ushers passed a letter to all of those assembled. It was his letter of resignation from the church. We literally and figuratively walked out toward our dream!

Chapter Summary

Perception helps you to see your dream; visualizing leads to passion and often courageous action.

Points to Ponder

Take time to think about what excites you. What sparks your energy and enthusiasm?

Chapter Six

Where Am I?

Am I Living My Dream?

"We can chart our future clearly and wisely only when we know the path which led to the present. " Adlai Stevenson

Have you ever gone on a road trip? The first thing you do when you look at the map or go to MapQuest, is to determine where you are starting from – where are we now? You then look at where you want to go. With this information, you get an idea of how long it will take, how far it is. You may be upset to know that you have a long way to go. Nevertheless, you do know. The first step to losing weight, a lofty dream, is knowing what you weigh now. Get on the scale! Those 20 pounds you thought you had to lose became 45 pounds!

Knowing where you are gives you the passion to get moving. It also helps you to gather an accurate assessment of what it will take to make your dream come true. It gives you a sense of discontent. You should be uncomfortable with where you are now .If you are comfortable with where you are now, you are more likely to remain comfortable. If, however, you really want to start moving toward your dream, this chapter is important to you.

Jewell thought she could only be a secretary. It was not until God placed a dream in her heart and spirit that she realized "where she was" was not "where she wanted to be". Her attitudes and beliefs changed and motivated her toward her dream.

Your dreams start where you are now. *Be honest* – We are at a different place within each aspect of life. We are closer to our dream and purpose in some and farther away in others.

Dorothy Height lived out her purpose from the days of her youth. If you are a young person reading this, what a wonderful adventure it is to discover your purpose and live out your dreams for the remainder of your life.

I dare say that most of us do not know what our purpose is until later in life. Some never do. Others become enlightened after a crisis or life change. There are also seasons in our lives that cause us to re-evaluate where we are and whether we need to "revisit" our dreams.

Our purpose remains constant: **to glorify God.**

When my husband died, I had to spend time alone with God. "What now, Lord?" I needed to acknowledge that I was entering a new, unfamiliar season of my life. The previous plan for glorifying God had shifted. I felt fulfilled in my dream and purpose as a partner to my husband. There was no regret, only a sense of thanksgiving to God for this season of service, love and joy. I also am thankful for the knowledge early in my life that my purpose for being on earth is to glorify God.

That purpose was expressed in loving my husband for thirty-four years and serving the people of the church and the community with the gifts, skills and abilities he placed in me. Therefore, when my husband died, I did not die. There were times, I must confess, when I felt so much grief that dying seemed a merciful choice. Not suicide, just dying.

I thank God! I knew in that transitional time God would lift me up and redefine His plans for continued service. The writing and publishing of this book is part of that plan. I thank Him for the renewed energy as I dream once again with my eyes wide open.

We must each discover where we are in order to perceive where we want to be (our dream).

Let's look a moment at God's question to Adam.

God says, "Adam, where are you?'

We all know that God knew Adam's location. He is God. This question was designed to cause Adam to examine and assess his purpose and relationship with God.

Adam was created to fellowship with God, to provide spiritual service to God, to take care of the garden, and to rest in the garden. As we know, Adam messed up. God used this question for re-focusing. God wants you to re-focus.

Where are you in your personal, professional, family, and spiritual life?

When you assess your location, you will discover that the tension between where you are and where you want to be will create a healthy energy that can propel you forward.

In his book, *The Path of Least Resistance*, author Robert Fritz tells of the tension produced by a rubber band when you pull on it and the release of energy and tension when you let it go. This is a good analogy to remember.

At the core of who you are, where you are and where you are going are your attitudes and beliefs.

What do you believe?

Belief: I believe that dreams can come true.

Impossible ---------Probable------------- Possible

Where do your beliefs fall on this scale?

Do you have confidence that your dream is possible?

If you have a dream of a lovely home, do you **really believe** that it is possible to attain? Your attitude and beliefs, your faith or your doubt, your "I can" or "I can't" will determine where you are. They are the bridge between where you are now and where you want to be.

Where you are	attitudes and beliefs Faith or doubt	where you want to be

Unexamined negative attitudes and beliefs can become bigger than your dream and then turn into obstacles. Your attitudes and beliefs are creating the world that you now experience and will experience in the future.

Common Reasons Why People Fail to Achieve What They Want

- Holding a belief that success is simply luck
- Not being able to change their thoughts
- Wasting attention on things they don't want
- Having no goals or dreams in life
- Not understanding that they have a choice
- No knowledge how the dreaming process works

The Boyds, Clint and Elaine were living the somewhat comfortable life. They were both functioning for almost twenty years in "corporate America", with college business degrees, a nice home, with a son and a daughter. Within a period of two months, they both lost their jobs. At stake was their standard of living, their lifestyle, their very existence. This was a time of decision and introspection. Six months before this, God had planted a "dream seed" in Clint. So when he and his wife lost their jobs, they began to first take the time to pray, retreat and have what they call a "gut check."

Their dream seed was to start their own business, realizing the gifts and skills they already had. During five days on the beach, they prayed, listened to God and examined themselves. "What do we always do? What arouses our passion? We write, we talk, we encourage, we train." At the same time, God was deepening their spiritual lives as Clint becomes a deacon in the church and Elaine takes the leadership in the Women's Ministry. They received the confirmation from God and decided to move forward with their dream. We will follow Clint and Elaine as they broaden their horizon.

Points to ponder

1. Write down your core or fundamental values.
2. **Where are you in your personal, professional, family, and spiritual life?**
3. Look and honestly examine whether your beliefs are strong or weak. (Notate any observations.)

Chapter Seven

Where Am I Going?

Am I moving toward my dream?

One of the greatest examples of a person living his life with purpose is in the Old Testament book of Genesis. In chapter 12, God told Abram to leave his country, his family, and his father's home for a land that He would show him. Abram was seventy-five years old with a wife and no children. He believed God and did as he was told .In chapter 13, God said to Abram (later named Abraham), "Open your eyes, look around. Look north, south, east, and west. Everything you see, the whole land spread out before you, I will give to you and your children forever. He left everything familiar and started walking.

Why?

He had a dream and God told him to follow that dream. He went looking for something he couldn't see while following a God he couldn't see. You may be the same – Your dream of graduating from college, owning a home and getting married may not make sense. **You may not know what you are doing but you can be sure that God's knows. "I know what I'm doing. I have it all planned out – plans to take care of you, not abandon you, plans to give you the future you hope for. "(Jeremiah 29:11) (MSG)** He knows where we are going even when we don't.

Abraham had a relationship with God and trusted Him. His trust moved him to obey and start toward his dream. His obedience was an act of total faith in God. You must move in the same confident way.

If you travel by car from Chicago to New York, you cannot see that far. You know that you will eventually get there if you are headed in the right direction and don't stop. Your headlights at night allow you to see only forty feet ahead of you. Yet you take the journey knowing that you will make it to New York.

There are some similarities and differences between driving to New York and achieving your dream. The dream process is not a destination. It is really the journey as well. It is a process that begins with one step or sometimes a "leap of faith".

One of my writing retreat spots was Negril, Jamaica. It was there that I saw a strong, young man climb to a platform at the top of a 50 ft. tree. He had a great audience of tourists. He waited until all eyes were focused on him. He then jumped with great abandon off this cliff into the rocks and ocean below. Of course, he had done this many times before. What was interesting, however, was that he inspired many of the same tourists to jump (from a lower level) - perhaps the first time for most .His leap, like Abraham's journey of faith, inspires us to dream, not always knowing how to get from **where we are** to **where we want to be.**

SO, how do we do this?

Well, back to the car example. In my car, there is a GPS (Global Positioning System). It is a navigational device that I can't do without. I am directionally challenged! I start out, not knowing how to get where I am going. I know my starting point, and I can place the address of my desired destination in the system.

Key points:

1. **You have to trust the system**. If you question the system and try to go 'your' way, you may get lost. The **Holy Spirit** is our GPS system. You must consult with Him before you begin your journey toward your dream. We don't know the path, but He does. There are times when I doubt that I am going right, but I trust the system.

2. **You have to get out of your driveway before it can engage and guide you**. You can't stay in the same place where you are now. Make the first step .Get going. Stop sitting around thinking about it! **Move!** You must have faith! You do your part, God does His part.

Hebrews 11:1 says," Faith is the confidence that what we hope for will actually happen; it gives us assurance about things we cannot see."

**Faith is the power to make things happen.
We must trust God.**

> *Trust GOD from the bottom of your heart;
> don't try to figure out everything on your
> own. Listen for GOD's voice in everything
> you do, everywhere you go; he's the one who
> will keep you on track.*   *Prov. 3:5-6 (MSG)*

**J. Oswald Chambers says, "Faith never knows
where it is being led, but it loves and knows
the One who is leading."**

Here we are on Resignation Sunday, 1977 at
the Pilgrim Emanuel Baptist Church in Nashville,
Tennessee. My husband has just read the letter
explaining why and when he would resign .It was
a gigantic leap of faith, not knowing where we
would meet the next Sunday or even if anyone
would come with us. There was no money, no
promise of support, only a great big dream.

My husband decided the new congregation
would be called the Temple Baptist Church. We
believed that we could do this, with God's help.
The dream came from Him. I told my husband
that I would play the piano and the children would
say, "Amen", and we would have church. God
did provide a place, Meharry Medical College
Learning Resource Center.

It was exhilarating, exciting and scary all at the same time. On the first Sunday of the newly formed church, my husband stood in the temporary 'office', peeking out the window and wondering out loud, "Do you think anyone is coming?." **Yes, they did come**. The choir was organized, the ushers were in their place, and we even had printed programs! The dream journey was beginning!

Chapter Eight

What's in my hand?
Exodus 4:1-5, 10-20

God is moving Moses toward his purpose. He is developing a leader in difficult times. There is the mass genocide of male babies. Moses is spared. He is young and untested. Moses knows that his purpose is to deliver his people, but doesn't know how to accomplish it. He goes ahead of God's plan. The next significant event, the burning bush, gets Moses' attention after forty years in the wilderness.

There are some lessons to be learned from him.

When living on purpose, don't bring up your past.

Say: My past will not hinder me. God called me.

Don't offer excuses, even if you don't have all the answers.

Moses offered excuses. He said that he could not talk well and had no experience. You can't opt out because you don't have all the answers. Answers come only in the process as you grow.

Don't disqualify yourself as a leader.

Moses asked, "How am I going to be the leader?"

People want - a person of integrity
-a person of their word
-one who can be trusted

You have these qualities already.

When God calls you, flow in what you know!

God asks Moses," What's in your hand?"

Moses looks at the stick, the staff in his hand. It was nothing unusual. All shepherds carried a staff to ward off wolves and other predators from the sheep. It was just a stick .God tells him to take it and throw on the ground. It becomes a snake. Moses ran; it scared him. God told him to take it by the tail. He picks up the very thing he ran from. God said it; Moses did it. There was no fear.

It becomes a staff again - an ordinary thing becomes an extraordinary thing under the power and authority of God. This is the same stick that was used to turn the Nile to blood, brought plagues and parted the Red Sea.

Final lesson from Moses:

Use what God has given to you. Don't complain about what you don't have. Don't define your dream by what you don't have. You may have:

-no education
-no money
-no friends/no connections
-no place to live
-no place to start a business

Use what you have to get what you need. Clint and Elaine Boyd realized that they had skills developed in their corporate world that would be useful in their own business. Rev. Michael and Eleanor Graves realized that what they had was each other and a mighty God.

What do you have? You have a dream and a mighty God who uses ordinary people to do extraordinary things.

On the *Today Show Broadcast,* on November 2, 2009, I was mesmerized by the true life story of Brenda Combs.

Brenda was living on the streets of Phoenix under a bridge.

She was the victim of a drive-by shooting. She was beaten up a couple of times, robbed once of her shoes while she tried to sleep. Her life was awful.

She was a drug addict.

She said, "I told myself, this is not God's plan for me. " She went from homelessness to now working on her Ph.D. degree as a teacher. She found her purpose – to become a positive member of society .She said that it was a long process. "I got involved with the church and I started singing and writing songs and journaling and just got involved, and I had a lot of support from my family, my friends and my church."

She tells others, "You can come from the bottom to the top" and "nothing is impossible." She now states that her purpose is to be the "best example of love and service to others."

You may think that you have nothing in your hand to begin your dream process, but God just needs an obedient and willing spirit. He will use your little "stick" to do miraculous work!

In 1879, Professor John F. Draughon, who was living in Adams, Tennessee, realized the need for business trained people. With very little capital, a horse, a wagon, and the teaching materials that were available at the time, he founded Draughons Practical Business College on wheels. He made a monthly circuit of towns in Northern Middle Tennessee and Southern Kentucky for several years before opening his permanent school in Nashville.

From this humble beginning and his business college on wheels, he started one of the largest chains of business colleges in the nation. At the time of his death in 1921, there were 38 business schools bearing his name. On January 1, 2010, the College changed its name to Daymar Institute and began offering bachelor of applied science degree programs.

Speaking of humble beginnings, I cannot omit the history of Bethune-Cookman University. In 1904, a very determined young black woman, Mary McLeod Bethune, opened the Daytona Educational and Industrial Training School for Negro Girls with $1.50, faith in God and five little girls for students. Throughout Dr. Bethune's lifetime, the school underwent several stages of growth and development. In 1923, it became a co-ed high school as a result of a merger with the Cookman Institute of Jacksonville, Florida.

A year later, the school became affiliated with The United Methodist Church; it evolved into a junior college by 1931 and became known as Bethune-Cookman College. In 1941, the Florida State Department of Education approved a 4-year baccalaureate program offering liberal arts and teacher education.

Dr. Mary McLeod Bethune was born on a farm near Mayesville, South Carolina in 1875, the 15th child of former slaves. She rose from humble beginnings to become a world-renowned educator, civil and human rights leader, champion for women and young people, and an advisor to five U.S. presidents.

She had a dream of opening her own school. That dream moved her eventually to Daytona Beach. Her dreams arose from seeing a need and then finding a way to meet that need. Mary McLeod Bethune's vision and legacy of faith, scholarship and service live on today at the school that she founded. Always dreaming with her eyes wide open and 'seeing' a need , she opened a hospital in Daytona Beach when a black student was turned away from the hospital. The nation was at war and needed all the resources available, regardless of color. Dr. Bethune saw the need to integrate the American Red Cross and Women's Army Auxiliary Corps.

As she made these dreams become reality, she relied on her faith and prayers for guidance and inspiration. She speaks to us today: "Without faith, nothing is possible. With it, nothing is impossible."

Here are two stellar examples of looking at what's in your hand and moving ahead with God- A man with a horse, a wagon and teaching materials and a woman with $1.50.

Never allow lack of resources to stop the progression of your dream! God's provision flows to a God-given vision!

What's in your hand?

<u>Points to ponder</u>

Take prayer time to examine what's in your hand. What "resources" do you already possess?

What makes you unique?

<u>Summary of Principle Two- Purpose</u>

Definition of purpose

Purpose is the **cognitive awareness** in cause and effect linking for achieving a goal in a given system. Its most general sense is the anticipated result which guides decision making in choosing appropriate actions within a range of strategies in the process. Purpose serves to change the state of conditions in a given environment, usually to one with a perceived better set of conditions from the previous state.

Translation:

Purpose is the **cognitive awareness**	*(Perception)*
In cause and effect linking	*(take a chance, make mistakes)*
for achieving a **goal** in a given system	*(making your dream come true)*

It's most general sense is the **anticipated result** *(faith through Holy Spirit)*

which guides decision making **(who I am, where I am , where I want to be, where I am going)**

in choosing appropriate **actions** **(goal-setting, prioritizing, persevering, possessing)**

within a range of strategies in the **process** **(overcoming obstacles, opposition)**

Purpose serves to change the state of **conditions in a given environment usually to one with a perceived better** set of conditions from the previous state. **You go from where you are to where you want to be (your dream)**

Principle Three

Partnership: Get Help With Your Dream

Chapter Nine

Choose and lead your group

Dreamwork Takes Teamwork

"A burning purpose attracts others who are drawn along with it and help fulfill it."

Margaret Bourke-White

Now that you have a dream and you know what your purpose is in having this dream, what's next? **The next step is to get help.**

A great example of people helping each other is **Ladies Who Launch**, a national company, the first new media company to provide resources and connections for women entrepreneurs. Women are launching businesses at twice the rate of men, and they are doing it primarily for lifestyle reasons–they want more freedom, flexibility, and creativity in their lives.

The **Ladies Who Launch** mission is "to make entrepreneurship accessible to any woman with a project, dream or aspiration to start her own business and be successful." We have found a definitive link between launching a business and higher self-esteem and happiness; it is our hope that women will come to Ladies Who Launch and take advantage of our trusted community, tools, resources and success stories and live their dreams.

Ladies Who Launch is a "feminine approach to launching dreams or goals, businesses and relationships," said Sheilah Griggs, leader of the new Nashville arm of the national company .It begins with an "incubator", an intensive four-week course limited to twelve women. These women are at different points in their dream.

"It can be a woman whose dream has always been to write a book, to someone like me, who said, 'I think I have an idea, something I want to do with our company.'" These women are helping each other. They share ideas freely; they work on each other's ideas. They realize that dream work takes teamwork.

In order to make your dreams a reality, you need partners. You need a team.

You need help in making your dream come true. You cannot do it alone and in a vacuum. Your eyes are now open; you see the dream, the vision. **Your next step is to help others see what you see**. You must find a group that has caught your vision.

Mother Teresa was in Phoenix, Arizona to open a home for the destitute. One of the largest and most powerful radio stations, KTAR in Phoenix, was represented by a reporter who asked Mother Teresa what he could do for her. He thought to himself as he was asking that question that she would respond by saying, " give me a donation... or get your radio station to give a donation"... or that she would ask for some free radio time so that she could publicize the event and raise money for the destitute. To his utter surprise, that was not her response. She looked at him in the kindly way, and she said to him, looking up from her back bent: "Son what you ought to do is find somebody that nobody else will love, and you love them."

It was too easy to give money. That was not catching the vision. The dream of Mother Teresa was to help the destitute, wherever they were and to love those that nobody loved. She wanted this reporter to catch the dream and become a partner in his own arena.

Your dream may involve meeting others' needs, starting a new business, financial security or being a successful leader in your ministry. Whatever it is, you have to get other people to help and cooperate. We live in such a competitive world, that cooperation is hard to find, especially if the dream is your dream and it will not necessarily benefit those helping you.

What is needed to make a dream come true, whether that dream is saving souls, leading people to live godly lives or, as in Mark's gospel, healing a paraplegic is **cooperation and partnership**. The goal of these four men was to get this man to Jesus. They knew that Jesus could heal him. That was the dream. They were not the ones needing the healing, but this one man on the stretcher.

This paralytic was suffering from palsy, more accurately, he was paralyzed. He was 'dead weight.' He had to depend on everybody to do everything for him; he had to be fed; he was helpless. His greatest dream was to be independent.

A crowd gathered, jamming the entrance to the house where Jesus was teaching. When they weren't able to get in because of the crowd, they removed part of the roof and lowered the paraplegic on his stretcher down in front of Jesus. Impressed by their bold belief, Jesus said to the paraplegic, "Son, I forgive your sins." He told this paralyzed man to get up, take his bed and walk. His dream was immediately realized with the help of his team.

Perhaps this is your dream – to be financially independent. You may be on welfare and desperately trying to live without assistance. You may feel completely helpless and trapped, but you still have that dream. You want to have your own home, your own car and be able to clothe, feed and educate your children.

Grab your dream and then get some help.

In the business world, getting help is called **networking.** There is power in networking. Surround yourself with like-minded people because being in business can be a lonely experience, especially in the early days of perception and formulating a plan. You will find that "two (or more) heads are better than one." You can create a service or product that is more productive and successful than thinking alone.

Look around you. Who is there to help? God has people waiting for you and your dream. They may not be the ones you thought would catch the dream. Don't be surprised.

After the initial anxiety of deciding to build a business and after three years of Clint's working in pharmaceutical sales to save enough money to begin, this couple began to see God's hand in sending those unexpected 'earthly angels' to help them. One of the first 'angels' was a mechanic who fixed their old Volvo (the gray ghost). He allowed them to pay him when they were able. There were many more. I was deeply moved by the story of an inmate at a prison facility who wrote a letter of encouragement to Clint, thanking him for a training he experienced. He sent in that letter $25. This may seem a small amount for most, but for this inmate, who made fifty cents per hour, it represented five weeks of salary. The 'earthly angel' was an encouraging partner to the Boyds. They later sent him back $50 to thank him for his seed money.

The Boyds are now functioning in their dream of a business. It is **Higher Ground Training, Inc.** They have worked with over 6,000 high school students, homeless people, ex-convicts, and business people, helping them to find balance in their lives and achieve excellence. As an added bonus, their family has changed during this process. Their children have become more aware of the importance of serving, the unimportance of money. There is "more compassion with fewer resources."

Success is no longer measured in terms of money. Success is now measured in intangible values. They have all become more resilient, no longer taking things "for granted." They know they have been chosen to carry out this mission, this dream. They have also grown spiritually and realized the importance of scripture memorization and journaling.

You can contact them at www.higher-groundtraining.com.

So far, we have **perception** (seeing the dream), **purpose** (realizing why you have a dream) and **partnership** (getting help with your dream).

Before you approach potential partners, you must have your dream clearly defined in your mind and on paper.

An exercise for you -

Write down on a 3x5 card and memorize what is called " elevator talk" – a 30 second description of your dream.

For example:

"I am starting a business that will allow you to take care of your dog even though you may

be out of town. I will make sure your dog is fed, walked and if necessary, housed temporarily for a small fee. This business will be in the next five years a franchise known for its attention to excellent dog care. I am looking for a few business partners. Do you know of anyone who may be interested?"

Dorothy Height- civil rights activist
"You can do something significant only by being a part of a collaborative, organized effort...a kind of unity that makes it possible of us to make an impact."

Now you are ready to choose your group.

In the Old Testament account of Judges, Gideon got up early one morning; all of his troops were right there with him. They set up camp at Harod's Spring. Gideon, one of the Lord's chosen, had a dream. **Gideon's dream was to win the battle against the Midianites**. He had an overwhelming task. Gideon had 32,000 men. Even with 32,000 men, he was still greatly outnumbered. Have you ever felt that way? No matter how much you have, you never have enough; no matter how much money you have, you don't have enough to accomplish your dream; when it comes to your friends you never seem to have enough to help.

God said to Gideon, "You have too large an army with you. I can't turn Midian over to them like this."

Why did God say Gideon had too many men?

God said, "they'll take all the credit, saying, 'I did it all myself '; and forget about me." God wants to get credit for this victory. He wants to get credit for your dreams coming true. You must not fall into the trap of giving yourself credit for what God will do. Many of us are guilty of that. We talk about good luck. "I had real good luck in starting my business." That makes God jealous because what you are experiencing is the blessing and favor of God, not good luck. We say, 'Oh, I just happened to be in the right place at the right time." **Not so!** It was God who put you in the right place at the right time. God doesn't want you to praise your circumstances or your situation. He wants you to give Him the credit. He wants to get the glory.

God's timing is perfect if you follow His lead. God told Gideon to make a public announcement: "Anyone afraid, anyone who has qualms at all, may leave Mount Gilead now and go home..." Twenty-two companies headed for home (22,000 men). Ten companies were left.

God said to Gideon: "There are **still too many**. Take them down to the stream and I'll make a final cut. When I say, 'This one goes with you,' he'll go. When I say, "This one doesn't go', he won't go." So Gideon took the troops down to the stream.

God said to Gideon, "Everyone who laps with his tongue, the way a dog laps, set on one side. And everyone who kneels to drink, drinking with his face to the water, set to the other side." Three hundred lapped with their tongues from their cupped hands. All the rest knelt to drink.

God said to Gideon, "I'll use the three hundred men who lapped at the stream to save you and give Midian into your hands. All the rest may go home."

Can you imagine?

On that day, Gideon's team was reduced to only 300 men. They were more powerful than the original 32,000 men because they were courageous, unselfish and dependent on God for the victory. **They won!**

God has to reduce us sometimes; reduce our physical power; reduce our material powers; sometimes God even has to reduce us in our church life so that we will not grow proud and arrogant and believe that it is our own strength, ingenuity, creativity or imagination that has brought us to where we are. When we ultimately have won the victory and our dreams come true, we will have to say, "Look at what GOD HAS DONE."

Some people brag, "I'm a self-made man." Since when do you know how to make a man?

Ask yourself: Who kept my heart beating last night while I slept? Your heart never missed a beat. **Answer:** Nobody but the Lord. Who kept my lungs inhaling and exhaling and blood cursing through my veins? Nobody but the Lord. Give Him the credit and praise. Learn to trust God with your dream and your team.

When God gives you a dream and you begin to choose your team, use these measures. Don't worry about how many you have. Trust God. Here are the important characteristics:

1. **Choose people with courage.** Let the scared people go home. Gideon allowed those who were scared to go home. 22 companies left him. That was 22,000 people. Gideon did not need scared people. Scared people are dangerous people. They will not only get themselves killed; they will get **you** killed, too. Many churches go through this 'purging'. As the

pastor, you can begin to wonder what God is doing. My experience is that God will help choose your team. He has some prostitutes on the street who haven't yet met Jesus but sends them to your side. God has some "winos" who are courageous. They are ready to throw down their bottle and ask, "How can I help you?" Then God will "clean" them up and make them the best team member.

2. **Choose unselfish people**. God told Gideon to take the remaining 10,000 to the brook and just let them drink water. You can tell a whole lot about people if you watch them. My pastor, Rev. Earl L. Harrison, Shiloh Baptist Church in Washington, D.C. told me never to read in the airport. He says that the best lessons are walking around you. Learn to be a student of human nature. Be a people watcher. God gave these same instructions to Gideon. So Gideon takes them down to the brook and watches. Those who go down to the water and are so thirsty they just throw their weapons down, get down with their head in the water, lapping... place them on one side. Those that go down to drink and get on one knee while still holding their weapon in one hand, dip

the water with the other hand, bringing the water up to their mouths – sit them on the other side. These are the warriors who are unselfish. They are not so preoccupied with their own need for water, but remain on guard. You don't want selfish people on your dream team. Selfish people only think of themselves. They are not willing to sacrifice for a dream. They always ask: 'What's in it for me?"

What about you as you form your dream team? God has people who will "catch your dream"; it will become their dream and they will move ahead with courage and selflessness, realizing that God can take a few people and make a mighty, victorious army.

In the formative years of the Temple Church in Nashville, the original partnership of Michael and Eleanor Graves was expanded to include two hundred and fifty-six other individuals who caught the dream and wanted to help. Some came alongside from a conversation at the gas station, some directly from 'the street'. Most were not 'traditional Christian' people, but people excited to be involved in a vision of something new that God was doing in the city of Nashville.

The Temple Baptist Church was made an official body on August 8, 1977 at the American

Baptist Theological Seminary. That Monday evening was warm and humid as people crowded with great excitement into the small chapel. Everyone could not get in the space, so some stood outside and peeped through the open windows as the statement proclaiming the formation of the Temple Baptist Church was read by the State Moderator, Rev. Nightingale. A resounding vote of "yes" was acknowledged, with some projecting their hands for a vote through the windows. The excitement, anticipation and joy were just as thick as the humidity that night. God was creating a new movement and everyone sensed His presence.

The next move was for Pastor Graves to form his team. There was no deacon "board" or trustee "board". There were, however, trusted men and women who came alongside him as advisors, partners, and encouragers. God assembled, through His Holy Spirit, a team of community people, bankers, politicians, construction laborers, teachers, domestic workers, doctors, and lawyers- people from all walks of life. All were inspired by a man of God with a dream! The Temple Church could not have moved forward without the partnership of many humble, hard-working, dedicated people of God. Some were poor, yet willing to take their 'corner' of this dream. There was no competition; only one anointed and appointed leader, Rev. Michael Lee Graves and one united family determined to glorify God and build His church. Without their faithful service and sacrifice, the Temple Church would not be the church it is today. They were courageous, unselfish people ready to move forward.

The dream team was in process!

Once you have chosen your team, you become the leader. As a leader, you need to know there are effective ways to work together. **Next chapter!**

Chapter Ten

Characteristics of
an effective team

There is the story of the football coach who was talking to his team before their first practice. He told them why they were chosen and what great players they were going to be. The players, eager and ready to begin practice, ran onto the field and then said," OK Coach, now what?"

In football, you really don't know what's next. The same goes for the functioning of your team. There are thousands of books describing teamwork and the details thereof. Just to get you going, here are some basics from the scriptural lessons we have been studying.

1. **Team members have their own distinct assignment** relevant to their abilities. In the Biblical account when the four men were carrying a sick man to the roof, in order to lower him to Jesus, each had to carry his own corner. We assume that each one was capable of carrying their own corner; otherwise, the paralytic would have fallen to one side or the other. When you gather your team, take time to discover their strengths and weaknesses. There are many inventories, for example, the Myers-Briggs, that help a team to function effectively. There are many churches that examine their pastoral staff using some measure of strengths and weaknesses. This team should function as a body functions, each part working together, yet having its own particular function. In the church, when everyone is in their place, there is more accomplished Pastor, deacons, nurses, ushers, and choir members are each in their respective places. You can get a job done and a dream realized when all involved pull their own weight and are in their own place. In the business world, the same is true. One partner may have technical skills and another managerial abilities. We can apply these

principles to a marriage. One spouse may be good at keeping the family financial record; the other person may be creative in ways to save money. Each partner has unique strengths and weaknesses.

2. **The team must move as one.** Once these assignments are made, **the team must move in sync.** Communication is vital. Surely this synchronized movement was necessary for the four men. It was also necessary for Gideon's three hundred men. Let's take a look at what they did. God told Gideon. "Get up and go down to the camp. I've given it to you." He overheard a friend who had a dream that Gideon had captured the camp. He immediately prayed to God. Motivated by God and this dream, Gideon divided his men into three companies. Each man had a trumpet and an empty jar with a torch in the jar. He said, "Watch me and do what I do. When I get to the edge of the camp, do exactly what I do. When I and those with me blow the trumpets, you also, all around the camp, blow your trumpets and shout, 'For God and for Gideon.' With your pitcher in your hand and your trumpet in your other hand, we are getting ready for the victory."

And so it happened! Gideon and his three hundred men blew the trumpets, and at the same time smashing the jars they carried. Can you imagine someone blowing before everyone else? It would have been disastrous! They then held the torches in their left hands and the trumpets in their right hands, ready to blow, and shouted. They were stationed all around the camp, each man at his post. Needless to say, the Midianites didn't know what to think. They were terrified! Not knowing what was going on, in confusion and fear, they ran. **Gideon had just a handful of men. God can take a little and make a whole lot!**

This summarizes the last point: The team must move as the leader instructs – not ahead of or behind the time. Many moves may not be understood, but your team must trust you as the leader. This means that the leader (you) must be in constant contact with God through prayer and devotion so that you lead as God leads you.

3. **The team must sacrifice.** In the gospel of Mark, these four men are working together to get one man to Jesus. Just imagine! They had to take time off from their jobs. They

had to lose at least one day's pay. They had to make the commitment to show up there on time and pick up their corner of the bed. They had to carry this man who was "dead weight". They had to stop along the way to feed him. He probably had no financial resources so they had a financial sacrifice to make. There is a sacrifice in being a part of a dream team. Needless to say, these men were unselfish and courageous as were Gideon's men.

What things do a leader and the team sacrifice?

- Individuality

Have you ever watched the Olympic sport of synchronized swimming? Every team member moves in exact movements that make each one look like a duplicate of the other. You see the team and not one individual. This takes much practice and discipline. The result is an Olympic medal.

A Christian cannot say, "I'm my own person." You are not. When you are in Christ, you are no longer your own, you no longer belong to yourself. You are Christ's person.

Most of the time we have to work as a team, no matter what we are doing – in a marriage, on the job or playing a sport. We are very seldom doing what we do alone. When we work with others, we realize who we are. Yes, we are unique individuals (God made us so!). However, we can't "do our own thing" when working as a team unless the team decides to do "your thing." In the church, many people believe that their 'vision' is just as important as the Pastor's vision. That may be so. If so, you need to start your own group of believers. There is only one leader, the 'Angel of the Church", the Pastor. **It is his vision** (as he follows Christ) that you work on as a church body. Your name may never appear on any list or on a plaque, but your contribution to the team is invaluable.

- **Less time for themselves**

Selfless devotion to a dream team requires less time for yourself. It may require less money for yourself. It may require putting your goals on the' back burner' until the group goals are met.

- **Ridicule**

How silly do Gideon's men look carrying into war a trumpet and a jar? Can you imagine people who may have heard of the plan and the subsequent ridicule? How crazy do four men look, carrying a paralyzed man up to the roof of a house?

When you move toward your dream, some people are going to say:

That's the stupidest idea I've ever heard!

You're going to do WHAT?

Are you out of your mind?

That will never work! No one has ever done that!

This dream team's commitment persisted through public ridicule. People in the Nashville community were heard to say, "You are stupid to give your money to that preacher!" "You are crazy, following that 'Jim Jones' and drinking Kool Aid. (Jim Jones was a leader who had a group of followers that willingly drank a poisonous drink, believing they would die and go to a better world.)

At work, on the bus, and often in their own homes, our members faced ridicule and derision. Some even had to justify their membership by physical defense. They were ready to fight for the dream!

Some outsiders came to worship as a result of hearing negative rumors. They decided to come and see for themselves. They saw the truth and joined the team! Some of our strongest advocates came out of curiosity.

- Not knowing the immediate future

Any planning is, at best, an estimate of how long it will take to start a new business, launch a new clothing line, get a college degree, or raise a family. What are unknown are the bumps in the road, the things that can easily de-rail or detour a dream. There is no way for a team to know the future.

- Finances

Many dreams begin with no money. Don't let the lack of finances deter you. **Money flows to a dream**. The new Temple Baptist Church Dream Team willingly took their places, gave of their money in a regular, consistent fashion. There were seven families (including the Graves family) who, by using their homes as collateral, risked losing their homes so that the church building could continue.

Undaunted, the Temple team would come and worship wherever we could assemble. We worshipped in school buildings, other facilities, sometimes moving weekly. (At this point, we had no money, no building, and no land.) The people caught the vision, and there was no turning back.

The road ahead was uncertain, filled with unseen challenges. You and your team must be willing to sacrifice individuality, less time for themselves, ridicule, not knowing the immediate future and finances .There is nothing more inspiring than to see a team working together for a common vision, a dream bigger than themselves.

We find a great partnership lesson from nature.

As geese take flight from the Canadian shoreline, they lift off from the water in squawking discourse. Yet, in a matter of seconds, a line begins to emerge from the mass of brown feathers. This line straightens, arches slightly, and then, as if on cue, bends sharply to form a perfect V formation. There is a very pragmatic reason for this: a flock of geese flying in formation can move faster and maintain flight longer than any one goose flying alone.

We have a lot to learn from these Canadian geese.

As each bird flaps its wings, it creates uplift for the bird immediately following.

- **By flying together in "V" formation, geese can fly further than if they fly alone.**

People who share a common direction and commitment to a dream can get where they are going quicker and easier because they are traveling on the energy of one another.

- **Whenever a goose falls out of formation, it suddenly feels the drag and resistance of trying to go it alone and quickly gets back into formation to take advantage of the lifting power of the bird immediately in front.**

- If we have as much sense as a goose, we will stay in formation with those who are heading in the same direction as we are.

- **When the lead goose gets tired, he rotates back in the wing and another goose flies in front.**

- It pays to take turns doing hard jobs with people or with flying geese. Dreamwork takes teamwork. The leader should share leadership and train those on his team to lead within their abilities.

- **These geese honk from behind to encourage those up front to keep up their speed.**

- We need to encourage each other, especially the leader.

Finally, when a goose gets sick, or is wounded by gunshot, and falls out of formation, at least two geese follow to help and protect him. They stay with him until he is either able to fly or until he is dead, and then they launch out on their own or with another flock until they catch up with their group. Even though there are sacrifices involved in a group making a dream come true, **there is also a beautiful sense of belonging and caring.**

If we have the sense of a goose, we will stand by each other, protect one another and sometimes even make new friends who are "flying" in the same direction. **In the business world, this is called SYNERGY. Synergy is a law of nature. Synergy is best explained as**, 'One plus one equals more than two'. Synergy helps you realize the value of others, and secondly, encourages you to find the right people. Synergy is a dynamic force in making your dreams come true. Use it and watch YOUR DREAM expand exponentially!

The fun is just beginning! Read on!

Chapter Eleven

How to deal with the obstacles and take calculated risks.

"…what thwarts us and demands of us the greatest effort is also what can teach us most."

Matthew Arnold

A s a dream team, there will be challenges and obstacles.

- You have everything in place, and you need more money than projected to start the production of your cosmetic line.
- The course that will allow you to complete your degree is not offered until next year. You are scheduled to graduate this spring.

- The trucks carrying the steel to continue the building process are roaring down the Temple Church driveway. This steel costs $150,000. It is COD(Cash On Delivery). The money in the church account is less than $500. A challenge.
- "You can't do that. Get a real job." Even well-meaning people can get in your way- On your way to your dream, people tend to get in your way They may even be people at your house...could be your husband, your wife, your son, your daughter, an auntie, an uncle, grandma, grandpa. Rather than encourage, they discourage you. An obstacle!
- You find out that in order to purchase a franchise, you need ten thousand dollars. An obstacle!
- You are working with partners who have different perspectives and ideas. You totally disagree on how to move forward on your project. An obstacle!

Once again, the four men in partnership, taking the lame man to Jesus had several obstacles. They first had to decide and agree on how to get to Jesus. With the large crowd, they chose the roof. But the roof was closed. So what are they to do?

What do obstacles do?

They make us stop and evaluate where we are and why we are pursuing this dream. Why are you doing this?

1. **Obstacles make us stop for a moment and think**. We not only think about our reason for continuing to follow this dream, but also how to deal with this obstacle.
2. **Obstacles can, if we allow them, stop the progress of our dream.** They can put us on hold. They can delay our **dream, especially if the obstacle seems"impassible."**Obstacles **can potentially kill our dream and stop us.**
3. **Obstacles hopefully make us think creatively" out of the box."** Imagine these four men, probably looking at each other and then at the roof. What do we do? Let's tear up the roof.

What an idea! There was no time wasted with a feasibility study, assessing the financial consequences of such action. There is a dream and together these men are together committed to making it happen.

"Nothing happens to anybody which he is not fitted by nature to bear." - Marcus Aurelius

4. **Obstacles may cause us to change our methods or ways to approach our dream**. You can turn your obstacles into opportunities. Many people know that what seems to be a "stumbling block" can be made a "stepping stone." There was a wonderful lady in our church, Mother Barbara Phillips who would say " **every bump is a boost.**"

5. **Some obstacles may cause you to wait.**

   The winning attitude is to wait and brainstorm to find a way to either go around the obstacle, go over it, or tunnel through the mountain created by it.

6. **Obstacles will make you pray.**

   When the steel for our new building was being delivered, we did not have the money to pay for it. The invoice said C.O.D. My husband, Deacon Seibert and Trustee Bill Mason were all outside , watching, kicking the dust around and praying. The two men asked my husband, "What are we going to do?" He replied, "We will just pray."

The building supervisor walked toward the three men and said, "The steel is all here. However, I know from experience that sometimes the steel does not fit. Let's wait until the steel is in place before we pay for it. I will give instructions to the steel company."

Can you imagine? There was shouting and rejoicing that day because God provided a way around a seemingly overwhelming obstacle.

"Determine that the thing can and shall be done, and then we shall find the way."
— Abraham Lincoln

I believe that for every obstacle or challenge, there is a way to overcome it! God knows the way. Go ahead and tear off the roof!! Move ahead with your dream!

TAKING CALCULATED RISKS

While your obstacle(s) have put you in a thinking mode, consider that you must take calculated risks to make your dreams come true. This can be the smartest and at the same time the dumbest thing. A smart risk is a calculated risk. You research alternatives and possible consequences and decide that the possible reward or payoff is worth it.

David, in the Bible, was eager to take the risk of fighting Goliath. He was a warrior who was insulted by Goliath's taunts toward his people and his God. He was also taking a calculated risk, aware of the rewards.

"The man who kills the giant will have it made. The king will give him a huge reward, offer his daughter as a bride, and give his entire family a free ride."

(MSG) I Samuel 17:25

How do you take a calculated risk? Having doubts about risk is natural, but you should not fear risks. This fear will only defer your dream. This fear, the opposite of faith, will paralyze you and prevent you from thinking creatively. We make choices on a daily basis that involve risk. Buying stock, changing jobs, getting married, sitting in a chair without examining its sturdiness are all risky. Every choice, including the choice to do nothing, involves some kind of risk.

The key to taking smart, calculated risks is to know what you want and the reward for the risk. Hopefully by now you have defined your dream. Your dream is what you want and its fulfillment is the reward.

Most people are not taking the risk of living their dream, but trying to please someone else or living just to make a living rather than the life they really want. The risk is worth the reward.

If your dream is to have more money, you might consider the dream of starting your own business. Taking a calculated risk means that you don't quit your job tomorrow with no money or prospect in sight. Your initial risks don't need to be so drastic. You take baby steps and begin saving the money needed to begin your business.

You don't risk everything. You also must learn from your failures when risks don't bring the desired result. You turn these failures into a positive experience by analyzing what went wrong. You then use this information to make a more informed choice.

Start taking small risks. Go home a different way from work; change your hairstyle; worship with people of another denomination or race. Risks involve stepping outside of your comfort zone. Taking small risks conditions you to take larger steps toward making your dreams come true.

A calculated risk taker stays alert to present and future trends. He/she analyzes the situation and makes realistic, specific choices. You must also take time and energy to analyze yourself as you manage your emotions. It is important not to waste time thinking about what negative things can happen. It is also important not to worry about what other people think. This is your dream, your risk. Keep pushing toward what you want and desire. Take the calculated risk.

My husband and I took a big risk, a 'leap of faith' when we left the comfort, security and familiarity of the church of seven years to begin the Temple Church. There was no promise of a place to preach or of a congregation to serve. There was the risk that no one would join us in this new venture. Many people called us 'crazy.' However, God **was AND IS faithful** and many joined us. We were pursuing a dream – a dream of a church, a group of people, who wanted to be involved in ministry that matters while loving God and each other. The risk was well worth the reward.

Taking a God-centered risk is not really a risk; it actually is the display of faith that pleases God.

You have overcome the obstacles standing between you and your dream. You and your partners have in a sense, torn up the roof and lowered the man down to his healing. The dream is being fulfilled.

The third principle, **Partnership,** is essential to the dreaming process. **You need help.** So you choose your group, unselfish people with courage; people who can 'see' your dream and are excited about helping you accomplish it.

Once you choose your group, you become the leader. As the leader, you need to know how an **effective team functions**. Team members each have their own distinct assignments, move as one, be willing to sacrifice individuality and time, risk ridicule and bear the insecurity of not knowing the immediate future.

As the leader, you realize there will be obstacles which could possibly stop you, but hopefully will create a momentary pause to stop and think creatively of ways to deal – perhaps by changing your approach, perhaps to wait and definitely to pray.

The leader of a 'dream team' must also know how to take calculated risks. The key to smart calculated risks is to know what you want and what the reward is for your risk. Taking a God-centered risk is not really a risk; it actually is the display of faith that pleases God.

Points to Ponder

"Teamwork is no accident. It is the by-product of good leadership."

John Adair

It is now time to prayerfully choose your team, your partners. Remember that it does not take a lot of people. It may be one or many. Pause and pray. God will place the right partners in your path. Contact them and give your "elevator talk." Gain a commitment to your team.

Principle Four

Possession: Go Get It!

Chapter Twelve

Possess your dream

You have chosen your team. Now you must go after your dream. Go get it. It's yours! YOU CAN HAVE IT! If it's more education, go get it. If it's a better relationship, go get it. Don't just sit there, go get it. Possess it!

The word, **possess** means not only to take hold of it, but also to take charge of it. It means to seize it so that it is not only a possession for you, but it's a possession for the generations that follow you.

If your dream is so selfish that it doesn't include anybody but you, it isn't a God given dream. God's dreams always include other people. There is no way for God to really bless you without somebody else getting blessed.

God blesses those through whom he can send a blessing.

So possess it! In the building of the Temple Church, we knew that 20 acres of land would not be enough for the generations and dreams to come. So we possessed 70 acres and we now have 100 acres. The interesting fact about our land was that it was once owned by Black farmers. Upon either losing or selling the land to White owners, they had no control over who would purchase the land. In the deed, there was the statement that this land was never again to be owned by people of 'African descent'. Look at God!

When a dream is yours, and you possess it, no one can stop the movement of God toward your dream.

God told the Israelites to go in and possess the land (Deuteronomy 11:19,24-26) and He gave them the boundaries: from the snowcapped mountains of Lebanon down to the Euphrates River over to the Mediterranean Sea, the great sea. The expanse of that land was 300,000 square miles. That's what God said they could have. Go in and possess it. At the height of Israel as a nation and a kingdom under the reign of Solomon, they only possessed 30,000 square miles. Here God has given them 300,000 square miles. Unbelievable!

Your dreams are probably unbelievably large. Don't be surprised. God has far more in store for you than you can think, dream or even imagine.

If you are satisfied with nothing, then you will have nothing. But if you want your dream, go get it.

How do you begin the process of possession?

The process begins with 'walking it off.'

You must map out in your mind what you want and then start 'walking it off' as a mental possessing of your dream. We're back to **perception,** the first principle.

Do you want a new house? Go and find your house and 'walk it off'. Your name is on it, but you've got to walk it off. If you need a new car and your car is broken down; go to the car dealership. Walk it off! It sounds silly and crazy; but there are some people who know that this works. The Israelites were told that everywhere their feet should tread would be theirs. They could have that land. After walking for forty years, they could have divided themselves up into walking teams and made sure that they walked out the whole land that God had promised them. Instead, they settled for 30,000 square miles. What are you settling for? People will tell you that your dream is too big; it's too tough; it's not possible; stop dreaming and get a real job. "

You have a dream that God has given you. You cannot afford to let that dream die. Possess it! Walk it off!

When the Temple Church was constructed, God gave us 28 ½ acres. We owned it, yet we did not yet possess it. There is a difference between owning it and possessing it. When we possess it, there will be not only a physical house of God for worship, but there will be a community of faith that will rise on these acres that will be a testimony to the power of Almighty God. When we came to this land, we walked off seventy more acres. This was the prophetic statement of my husband in 1990. Today the Temple Church has possessed and owns over 100 acres and there is a beautiful sanctuary with a vibrant community of faith of over 4,000 people. On August 1, 2010 we shredded the mortgage on the church, becoming a debt-free congregation! It started with a dream, people willing to partner with the dreamer and then going after the dream.

One thing you must realize is there are people who are watching you and believe **if you can do it, they can do it.** You must have enough faith to say, *"If I can walk it, God can give it."*

Just start walking. God will give it to you. Walk in faith. Walk and believe; walk and trust; walk and obey; walk and possess!

A plan for possession:

1. **Grab a dream** that is bigger than you. Perceive it. Think of people who have hurts and human needs. Robert Schuller says, "Find a need and fill it; find a hurt and heal it."
2. **Write it down**.
3. **Break it down into small specific steps. Example**: *I want to be famous.*
   - *I want to star in a movie*
   - *I want to go to three auditions every week*
     - *I want to move to New York*
     - *I want to save $5,000 to move*
       - *I want to work overtime / a second job*

4. **Give yourself deadlines for each step to beat procrastination.**

5. **Brainstorm all possible ideas.** Are there different ways to achieve your dream? Write down all possibilities, no matter how crazy or impossible. *Go to acting school, get into reality show.*
6. **Implement your plan. Start now.**
7. **Create benchmarks or ways to measure your progress. Review from time to time. Evaluate effectiveness. Are you getting results?**
   I know I am famous when I appear on network television.
8. **Use positive affirmations.** *I am unique, somebody special. I know I can...*
9. **Persist, be patient.** *You may have to switch to contingency plan(s). Learn from mistakes.*

Principle Four

Possession: Go get it

Chapter Thirteen

Remember

Don't forget:
1. **God has brought you this far.**

There is empowerment in taking a moment in the process of making your dreams come true to remember what God has already done for you.

The Israelites had experienced God's protection and provision in a miraculous way. They saw with their own eyes how God buried Pharoah's army in the Red Sea. This allowed them to walk through on dry land and when all of them had passed through the midst of the sea, the sea closed back in and covered the chariots of Pharoah, the horsemen and the soldiers. They saw how God took care of every need in the wilderness, feeding and clothing them.

When you have already seen God work in your life, **you must** go in the direction of your dream, knowing that God can and will perform more miracles on your behalf.

As you truly mentally and actually possess your dream, create a journal of God's goodness to you in the past.

This goodness is not all in material things, but also in health, strength, family, influence and even in the fact that you now realize you have a purpose, and partners in your dream process. Take time to thank God for bringing you this far. Thank Him for making, as our foreparents say, "a way out of no way."

Jewell and the Boyds talk about the importance of journaling as they progressed toward their dream. This helped them chronicle and remember God's guidance. One of my favorite hymns is "All The Way, My Savior Leads Me." The words speak to my spirit: "All the way my Savior leads me; what have I to ask beside? Can I doubt His tender mercy, Who thro' life has been my Guide? "There is great comfort and assurance in remembering that your Savior has been leading you and will continue.

2. **You haven't done this on your own.**

God also had Moses to remind the rebelling Israelites of the time when the ground upon which they were standing opened up and swallowed up Pharoah's men, their wives, their children, and their tents - everything they had. In a moment, it was all gone.

Moses shows us how to remember that as you go into this new land God has given you, be faithful to Almighty God. **Remember you haven't done this on your own**. It has not been your hand; it has not been your ability; it has not been your skill; but it has been God who has brought you safe so far. You are not self-sufficient. You must always acknowledge the source of your blessings. Can you think now of how God has already blessed you?

Where you are and where you are going is a gift from God. Your dream is a gift from God.

As you move forward in possessing your dream, pause to thank God for his provision and protection so far. This spirit of gratitude will propel you forward toward your promised goal.

3. To possess, you must obey God, Love Him and trust Him to fight your battles for you. You must develop the mindset of total dependence on God.

Faithfully obey all these commands I'm giving you. Love the LORD your God, follow all his directions, and be loyal to him. Then the LORD will force all these people out of your way. Then you will take possession of the land belonging to people taller and stronger than you."

The Israelites were about to possess the land promised to them – their dream land. But in this land were people taller and stronger. Their dream was looming large. The only way they were going to make it was to depend on God.

4. God cares about your dream

A woman saw a beautiful necklace. She purchased it and put it away. She married and kept it in a safe place believing that one day she would give this necklace to a granddaughter.

As she had children, she enjoyed them as they grew and became adults. Her daughter grew, got married and had a daughter. What joy there was! Now a grandmother, this woman knew that it was time to tell this young granddaughter of her plan. As a gift to her granddaughter for completing her college degree, she promised her this beautiful, expensive necklace.

The young lady loved the necklace and kept it in her mind. As she grew older, her dream was one day to own that necklace. She could see herself wearing it. She could feel it around her neck. She could hear the compliments of those who saw it and she could see the love and satisfaction on her grandmother's face.

So she worked hard! She had ups and downs in school. Many times it seemed as though she wouldn't make it. However, she kept going. On graduation day, her grandmother called her and said, "I've got your necklace – all you have to do is come and get it." She just had to **possess** it. It was always hers, but she had to work for it. Grandma said, "I had this for you even before you were born. I have held it for you. Come and get it."

That is what God tells us: "I have my eyes on you." You have God-blessed eyes; you have ideas and thoughts expressed as dreams. You've gathered people to help you; you haven't given up, now come and get it. At the end of the process, it will be yours. Go in the direction of your dream!

The little boy, David, had a dream of defeating this huge giant, Goliath. He had a God-given dream that would bless not only him, but also his people and his descendants. David realized his total dependence on God.

He did not have the resources to fight this giant. All God needed was a slingshot! He had no armament. He did not even have the physical prowess. It seemed to be an impossible dream. And yet, he possessed it with the knowledge and trust that God would make it happen.

Look at what he said:

> "I come at you in the name of GOD-of-the-
> Angel-. Armies, the God of Israel's troops,
> whom you curse and mock. ⁴⁶This very
> day GOD is handing you over to me. I'm about
> to kill you, cut off your head, and serve up
> your body and the bodies of your Philistine
> buddies to the crows and coyotes. The whole
> earth will know that there's an extraordinary
> God in Israel. ⁴⁷And everyone gathered here
> will learn that GOD doesn't save by means of
> sword or spear. The battle belongs to GOD—
> he's handing you to us on a platter!"

1 Samuel 17:45-48
(New International Version, ©2011)

What a statement! What an affirmation of faith!

His faith was based on his relationship with God and on his past experience. He was a shepherd boy who had faced challenges before. God allowed him to kill bears and lions with his own hands. He remembered God's protection in the past, just as the Israelites were told to remember God. With this attitude of remembrance and gratitude, David went against Goliath. He told Goliath what God was going to do. He spoke it first. He then used what small resources he had and God did the rest. As you know, Goliath miraculously fell to the ground and David's dream did come true!

A crucial step in possessing your dream is the acknowledgement that you need God to make your dreams come true.

> *God particularly pours out his blessings upon those who know how much they need him.*
> ROBERT HAROLD SCHULLER

David needed God.
David had a strong relationship with God.
You must have a strong relationship with God.
Ask God to bless your dream to fruition.

> *"Never undertake anything for which you wouldn't have the courage to ask the blessings of heaven."*
> GEORG CHRISTOPH LICHTENBERG
> (1742–1799)

What does it mean to have God bless our dream?

The word bless means to give success, prosperity. This blessing is provided within the context of a unique relationship with God. God made a promise and commitment to Abraham to bless his offspring in Genesis. But each generation and each Israelite had to personally accept that relationship by faith. Our generation must accept that relationship.

You must accept that relationship.

You must also choose to follow the moral and religious pathway God laid down in Moses' law. It is the path that leads to a blessing or a curse.

> *I've brought you today to the crossroads of Blessing and Curse.*
> ***The Blessing**: if you listen obediently to the commandments of GOD, your God, which I command you today.*
> ***The Curse**: if you don't pay attention to the commandments of GOD, your God, but leave the road that I command you today, following other gods of which you know nothing."*
> (Deuteronomy 11:26-28 The Message Bible)

We have a choice of blessing or curse. **What is a curse?** A curse is when you are weakened and limited. You are in some way bound and unable to do what you otherwise could do.

In summary, possess your dream. **Go get it! Possession** involves realizing that you need God. Therefore you must have a relationship with

Him and ask for His blessing. You have a choice of blessing or curse. However, choose blessing; listen obediently to the commandments of God and then He will be with you and do miraculous things in your life.

Principle Five

Perseverance: Hang in there

Chapter Fourteen

Encourage yourself and don't give up.

So now, you are in the process of possession. The next step and principle is *perseverance*.

Perseverance is the steady persistence in a course of action, a purpose, a state, etc. especially in spite of difficulties, obstacles, or discouragement.

Do you have dreams that seem to be on hold? You have your dream, you know your purpose, your partners are working together, you are possessing your dream and yet nothing is happening.

- You've laid out your plan that in four years you were going to do a certain thing, but the delays of life have put you and your dream on "pause."
- It has been four years and now you are forty years old.
  All the things that you wanted to accomplish by the time you were forty are a long way from being done.
- You are single, with no husband. Your dream was to be married with three children by now.
- You are working in a job that you don't like, and yet you can't quit because you've got to eat and feed your family. You feel discouraged and locked in.
- You have stepped out and have started your own business, but the economy has taken a downward turn and your business seems to be going under.

The Currys: A Story of Perseverance

Sidney and Saundra Curry always had the dream of owning their own company. The path to their dream had many detours, delays and discouragements.

They vividly recall a session with their pastor, Bishop Michael Lee Graves, when they were somewhat "stuck." Bishop told them to "get off the ramp and get on the road." So they did! Sidney shares this memory of Pastor's words as if it were yesterday. Today, whenever there appears to be a delay in making a decision, he falls back on those words of advice.

Their first venture, *Impressionable Events*, an event planning company, did not succeed. Their second experience, a restaurant, *Visions*, in partnership with a major restaurant chain, never got off of the ground.

A third company, Curry & Buckingham Enterprises or CBE, a restaurant training and consulting firm was designed to train individuals in all areas of restaurant management through consulting, videos and training modules . Money was being made, opportunities were surfacing and things were looking promising by the day. Although successful, it did not advance their dream as Sidney and Saundra both envisioned. Wherever they were being led by God, they knew upon arrival, it would bear their names, social security numbers and nomenclature coupled with their vision, purpose and passion. In hindsight, they both agree that CBE yielded invaluable lessons and prepared them well for what was to come.

Throughout this period of **almost ten** years, they never gave up and kept seeking. There were times of discouragement and what seemed to be barriers of entry. Sidney said, "We never lost our vision of victory. We never took our eyes off of our 'North Star.' " 2 Corinthians 4:8-9 says that, "We are hard pressed on every side, yet not crushed; we are perplexed, but not in despair; persecuted but not forsaken; struck down, but not destroyed." What others perceived as failure, they believed were opportunities to learn and build relationships with people in financial circles, especially bankers and investment counselors. Saundra, a banker herself, was constantly amassing knowledge, sorting and simplifying complex concepts. Her husband calls her the I.Q. (intellectual quotient) of their team. He considers himself the E.Q. (execution quotient) of their team. Somehow, God balances every team for maximum productivity. Simply put, Saundra draws up the game-plan and Sidney executes the scoring drives with many ending in a touchdown. They quickly learned how to stay in their own lanes where they knew how to drive the best. Sidney jokes that it's hard to imagine Saundra out on the field " juking, stiff arming, cutting, spinning and leaping into the end zone to score!"

After many "learning experiences", the vision begins to become clear. They both discovered that the dream was not in restaurant training and consulting. They also realized that making money as a primary goal can get you the wrong road, the wrong journey. Financial success is far different than purposeful success, though it is easy to feel as though you've finally arrived at your destination upon scoring sizeable financial contracts. **Your real purpose will go far beyond you, your family and your company**. Sidney and Saundra firmly believe that when one gets lost in the service of others, they will surely find themselves and their purpose. Once your purpose is realized, go full speed ahead! There will surely be others near and far that might state otherwise including, family, friends, colleagues, coworkers, etc. When Sidney and Saundra both left their full-time jobs, 2000 and 2001 respectively, to start their fourth and present company, Buckingham Curry Holdings, LLC or BC Holdings, LLC, most asked them to reconsider, be more conservative and take it slow; we often heard, "it's just too risky for both of you to leave at the same time."

Be careful to stay the course that God placed you on no matter how dark the cloud, wide the river, high the mountain, or low the valley may be in front of you. Delaying the journey or taking the wrong road could easily invite failure aboard and expend valuable time and resources needed to complete your journey. Sidney firmly states that delay is often the enemy of progress." When God sends you on a journey, be assured that you are more than adequately prepared to deal with any storm cloud that may rise. You have all the tools you need in your toolbox to fix any problem, starting with Him. We're made in God's image, which means we are destined to be great, from the start of our journey. No individual ever made it from good to great or greatness by staying in their comfort zone." They decided to get out of theirs.

Saundra resigned from the bank. Amazing circumstances at that time could have caused second thoughts. America had just sustained and been traumatized by a terrorist attack. The day was September 11. They both knew that, although the timing seemed wrong, there was no turning back. They had to close out negativity, overcome uncertainty and seize opportunities. Warren Buffet said it best when speaking to potential investors: "There will always be uncertainty in the world; don't let that reality spook you from seizing opportunities." Lightheartedly, remembering their past, Sidney went on to say : " We've had some pretty spectacular events happen to us in the fall and winter seasons of the year.., the birth of our children, our divine meeting and the start of their company…so why stop now, we're on a roll! "

The Curry's state that with 71% of America living paycheck to paycheck, financial distress reasonably sets into our households forcing people to lose focus on everything, but money. As a banker and now as CEO of BC Holdings, LLC Saundra saw first-hand where, if folk did not have money, their focus points inward, leaving little time for the service of others. Chasing the 'almighty dollar' as the song goes, instead of chasing "almighty God". Our children grow up in families that are stressed, depressed and in a mess about and over money. Employees are not as productive or performance-driven; citizens are not as community-focused; churches are not as financially fit and our children become generationally dependent.

Sidney and Saundra knew the order and how tall it was - **Financial Healing: Changing the way one thinks about money through education, exposure and understanding.** They also had to foster discipline into the equation. Our country, made up of families, children, churches, schools, corporations and employees, needed a paradigm shift from consumers to investors, a transformation from spenders to wealth builders. **. How much is your signature worth or what is your net-worth** are very common questions the Currys ask class participants who attend their sold out sessions across the country each and every week. Wearing your wealth, driving your wealth, living in your wealth to impress the court of public opinion is shallow and over-rated and has far less gravitas than building wealth, which one cannot see outwardly. Therefore, self-approval, self-confidence, self-motivating, self-control, self-discipline and self-satisfaction had to be a part of the "understanding" equation.

The vision had been realized and clarified and the task at-hand, like most God-ordained purposes, was large. As they saw it, this was a clear indicator that they were on the right road. The second sign was the incredible feeling of sacrifice. Because you now know your purpose, do not think that the road will become easier to travel. That's exactly when trouble really shows up. Sidney and Saundra ran into numerous roadblocks, inclement weather, potholes and detours financially and otherwise. Sidney put his pride in his back pocket and got a second job during the night hours after leaving BC Holdings each day, while Saundra continued full-time with BC Holdings. For two years, they traveled those rough waters. They frequently told themselves, "If you are not focused, how can you achieve what God wants you to do?" During these times, you have to grind it out and work harder, stay alert and be careful who you allow into your presence. Be sure to keep you full coat of armor on during your journey and keep a watchful eye.

Stop after stop, so many people commented that Saundra had such a gift in clearly explaining the easy way to build wealth and improve their overall financial understanding for them and their families. People felt less stressed and were hopeful towards a new beginning, a new way of thinking. At the same time, her personable and "pleasantly persistent" husband was continuing to network and build relationships. BC Holdings was providing their services and winning solutions to corporations, universities and local schools during the early periods of their business. However, they constantly sensed the effect of the recession immediately following September 911tragedy on their own business, in addition to their clients' businesses as well. Ultimately, corporations could no longer appropriate monies for this type of discretionary spending.

This large storm cloud eliminated a significant portion BC's profits. The Curry's first turned **to prayer** and then to the IQ of the business to strategically navigate their journey through this storm. One might ask, "Will the road ever get easy?" We simply respond that storms are an important part of life. Those who learn how to adjust and deal with them will most likely reach their destination.

Saundra steered BC Holdings, LLC towards the benefits gained from being a veteran-owned company. Sidney is a combat military veteran serving during the Gulf War. She realized that the government's budget was quite different from that of corporations in the private sector. Once again, their perseverance paid off. After not one or two, but three trips to Las Vegas in three successive years they found success again. They met with people that produced a partnership and alliance that allowed them to help federal civil servants in small group settings achieve their goals of financial wellness and healing. So in a time of recession, they found a recession-proof alternative: the federal government.

Sidney initiated this connection literally through an "elevator talk" when leaving his hotel room with a New Mexico state legislator! Of note, this was far from the exhibitor hall where business opportunities were to be conducted. One never knows when or how opportunity knocks, but must always be tastefully persistent and ready." If you flaunt it properly, they'll want it properly," Sidney says.

This inspiring couple says, "In the end, we win." In September 2011, the company will celebrate its 10 year business anniversary! They now travel extensively, not only making money, but more importantly changing lives. Their company, Buckingham Curry Wealth Builders, creates and delivers financial wellness programs and services to companies, colleges/universities, high schools, training organizations, government entities and non –profit organizations. Their largest customer is the federal government (Department of Defense) where they are making a direct impact on national security, which they add, was picked up in the middle of a storm! In their hearts, they know that financial healing is not a lost cause, but simply a cause not yet won; and at every stop, they are winning the cause.

The company has seen success on many fronts boasting a host of clients including Fortune 1000 companies and has been endowed with many awards including the Nashville Incubation Center Business Award, congressional recognitions for performance and most recently named the 2010 Tennessee Supplier of the Year, (TMSDC). The Currys are also very active in the community and giving back is a huge part of their personal and corporate values. They are members of the Temple Church, Nashville, Tennessee and are living their dream as they continue to follow their "vision of victory". They based at 114 Canfield Place, Suite B-9, Hendersonville, TN 37075.

How to Deal With Discouragement

Discouraged. Have you even been discouraged?

If your answer is yes, you're in good company because David was discouraged. Legend has it that on the day the devil was asked which of his weapons he would give up and which he would retain, the devil thought about it for a moment and said, "I will give up all my weapons but one and that is the weapon of discouragement. I'll just use that weapon to keep believers from doing what they need to do."

And so the devil decided that he was going to keep his weapon of discouragement because, he said, in this legend, "if only I can persuade men and women to be thoroughly discouraged, they will make no further moral effort and then I shall be enthroned in their lives..."

Everyone at one time or another is discouraged. Some of us have been discouraged by losses. Losses come in all shapes and sizes. Sometimes we are discouraged because our hopes have been hobbled and our dreams have been dashed.

David is a man at this point of discouragement. He is at low tide, in a valley. David is at the lowest point in his life. His dream has been delayed. He was anointed by Samuel, the prophet, to be King of Israel. Years have gone by and still he is not on the throne. David is discouraged. Sometimes discouragement comes from delays.

Have delays discouraged you?

David is not only discouraged by delays, but he is also struggling and is running for his life. He is running from the King, Saul, who is trying to kill him. Saul is chasing him all over the countryside. He has spies out looking for David. So David is discouraged not only because he is not king, but also because the present king is chasing him.

He is constantly struggling for his life,

Things in his life have gone from bad to worse. Sound familiar?

He hired himself out as a mercenary to his enemies, the Phillistines. David is in such bad shape economically, spiritually and every other way, that he actually goes to his enemy for a job. He gets hired, but one of the Phillistines remarked," We don't want him. Isn't that the man Saul is after? Isn't that the one who defeated our Goliath? We don't want him on our side. He may betray us."

As soon as he gets the job, he is fired.

Can you feel his discouragement? He is excited; he's happy; he's got a job. Then he hears, "YOU'RE FIRED."

He goes back to Ziklag and things get even worse. Upon arriving in Ziklag, he discovers that the Amalekites have come and kidnapped the women, sons and daughters, including David's wives.

Things have gone from bad to worse.

David's men, who really love him, are ready to stone him out of their anger and discouragement. There are no encouraging words coming from them.

David has to encourage himself.

There are times when there will be no one there to encourage you. There are times when you must talk to yourself.

You must say to yourself: **BE ENCOURAGED!**

You may be down today, with no money – **BE ENCOURAGED!**

You may be facing seemingly insurmountable odds – **BE ENCOURAGED!**

Notice that David did not encourage himself by wishful thinking. He did not close his eyes to the problem. He knew wishing would not make it better. Neither did David attempt to stoically look at the matter by thinking, "If I'm strong enough, if I'm man enough or if I'm bold enough, I can get through this."

David had to let God in on the situation. David had to remember "The Lord is my shepherd, I shall not want." (Psalm 23:1)

You must remember and affirm who God is and how he has helped you in the past.

David called for the priest and told him to get the ephod. The ephod was a vestment worn by the high priest. It was used by David to get advice and direction .He then had to wait on the Lord.

When our dreams seem to be on hold, we must not get discouraged. We must go to God in prayer, encourage ourselves and then wait on God.

After praying and waiting on God, David, after three days, got back what he lost. He also got back what he never had. His situation turned around. If you just wait on God, he'll turn your situation around. If you just trust Him, he will turn it around.

(Thoughts adapted from Sermon: Day of David's Discouragement- Pastor Michael Lee Graves - I Samuel 30:1-8)

We often wonder if we are the only one with days of discouragement.

> "Every day was a struggle emotionally for me; feeling that I wasn't good enough. I couldn't understand how the Lord was using me..."   Jewell

In his book, *Peaks and Valleys,* Dr. Spencer Johnson says that it is natural for all to have peaks and valleys. We must find within ourselves the ability to see the "good" in "bad" times. If you don't learn in the valley you become **bitter**. If you do learn in the valley, you will become **better.**

One way to go through the valley is to follow your vision of the peak you want to be on – your dream .He calls it a "sensible vision". We go from peak to peak, through the valley. **On the peaks, we celebrate life. In the valleys, we learn from life.**

We must be aware of arrogance disguised as confidence when we are on the peak. We must also be mindful of fear disguised as comfort in the valley.

Another thought is to realize that you are not defined by your peaks and valleys.

When you reach a peak in the dreaming process, there should be humility and gratitude, realizing that it was not your genius that got you there. This energizes you. It is this same energy that helps you to be grateful for the lessons you learned in the valley. As a rocket heads for the moon, it will be off target 90% of the time. If it is off even one degree, it will miss. Yet, it doesn't miss. How is this?

There is a constant correcting on the course. In our journey and process of dreaming, we will constantly be checking with reality.

The questions to ask:

Is what I'm doing raising or lowering my energy?

Am I getting results?

Am I peaceful?

There should be energy from both peaks and valleys dependent on how you look at them. Many people think of this as a bad time, a valley experience. Losing a job, losing a home, living from day to day, and scraping to make ends meet can be valley experiences.

But what can we learn?

Perhaps we learn how to make better use of the money we have. We reduce our reckless and unnecessary spending. We learn how to have fun without spending money. We have more time to spend with our family and gain perspective on what's most important.

Look for lessons.

Be grateful on the peaks and celebrate with humility. Learn in the valley and don't be afraid and get comfortable as you head toward your sensible vision of what can be – your dream.

"But the land you are about to cross the river and take for your own is a land of mountains and valleys;

As I am writing this chapter, I am looking at the ocean. I am watching as it ebbs and flows. Over several hours, the water rises and it reaches a high level. This is the high tide. A tide is a repeated cycle of sea level changes.

It reaches its highest level and stops at high tide. The tide reverses direction and then begins to recede and fall over the next several hours during the ebb tide. The level stops falling at low tide.

High tide. Low tide. Dramatic changes. There are organisms that live in this intertidal environment. They must **adapt** to this highly variable and often hostile environment in order to survive and thrive. **Some even exploit these conditions.** There are changes in temperature, salinity and pH of the water, moisture (high and low), dissolved oxygen and food supply. There are some organisms that must withstand and survive high water pressure as the waves dash against the shore to prevent being washed away.

So how do they survive? They **adapt.** Many burrow (like clams) in the sand. Some live under rocks or attach themselves to rocks (like barnacles and mussels). Some, such as snails, have protective shells.

Even nature teaches us that life has its high and low tides, its ups and downs.

Life is filled with ups and downs. **It is filled with good and bad.** It is filled with joy and sorrow, but you can make it because you are not in this thing all by yourself.

Our adaptation comes from knowing and trusting a God who is our shelter, our rock under which we can hide, our shelter in the time of storm.

We have a relationship with God, who helps us in every situation.

God is our refuge and strength, a very present help in trouble.

Psalm 46:1-3
(American Standard Version)

How did Jewel adapt?

"Every morning, I placed signs all over the bathroom wall – 'I can do all things through Christ, who strengthens me', 'Trust God with the process', etc. I had them on my refrigerator; I had them on my computer, the mirror in the bathroom. Every morning after my prayer time, I would walk through the apartment saying, 'I can do all things...' ,'greater is He that is in me...', all the things I had learned at the Temple Church."

Points to ponder

Draw on a sheet of paper a horizontal straight line. This line represents your life from birth to now. Chronicle your significant life events by a vertical line. After doing this, decide whether each of these events was an 'up' event or 'down' event. If it was an 'up', place a dot above the line. If it was a 'down', place a dot below the straight horizontal line. Connect the dots and see what pattern emerges.

Examine to see if there are more "ups" than" downs".
What did you learn from each one?
What was your help in your ups and downs?
What scriptures, affirmations are important to you?

God cares about your dream

As a child, can you remember running to a new, unfamiliar playground. The children around you were not your 'friends'. The swings and slides were higher than what you were accustomed to. It just felt uncomfortable. Then, all of a sudden, you would hear your mother's voice. "I've got my eyes on you – I'm watching you!"

What an assurance! You then began this new adventure knowing that you would be safe.

The great preacher, Rev. Charles H. Spurgeon, has a sermon, "Canaan on Earth", delivered on December 30, 1855, that gives wonderful insights into the following scripture.

> *"But the land you are about to cross the river and take for your own is a land of mountains and valleys; it drinks water that rains from the sky. It's a land that GOD, your God, personally tends—he's the gardener—he alone keeps his eye on it all year long."*
>
> *Deuteronomy 11:9-11- The Message Bible*

He states: "True religion makes a difference not only in a man, but in a man's condition; it affects not only his heart, but his state – not only his nature, but his very standing in society… My habitation is now guarded by Jehovah my position in this world is no longer that of a needy mendicant – I have become a gentleman-pensioner on the providence of God; my position, which was that of a bondslave in Egypt , is now become that of an inheritor in Canaan."

Your relationship with God now affords you a new "position."

The background of this scriptural passage helps us to understand this new "position" and how it helps you move toward possession of your dream.

In Egypt, the Israelites had to work very hard to grow anything because Egypt is a desert land with little or no rain. Any water had to be irrigated in by artificial reservoirs. The Nile River would overflow its banks, cover the land and provide water for these reservoirs. Then the water would flow through canals to the land.

The Nile was their source.

Spurgeon preaches, "Some rely upon what they call chance – (a river the source of which, like the source of the Nile, is never known) and though continually disappointed, they still persevere in trusting to this unknown stream."

Many people feel that making their dreams come true is by chance or by luck. They think they must "be in the right place at the right time." You hear from them "I just got lucky," "I played my cards right." There is no doubt that dreams do come true in this fashion. However, this scripture makes an important and pivotal paradigm shift. He goes on to elaborate that others, in a more sensible mode, rely on hard work and honesty. Certainly, hard work and honesty are very important.

But to Christian, what supersedes all of this is relying on scripture.

This Canaan, the promised land, a place flowing with milk and honey, their dream land, will be a place where, according to Spurgeon's interpretation

"thy mercies come not from the hand of chance; thy daily bread cometh not so much from thy industry **as from thy heavenly Father's care…**"

There is a certain" drive" one has as they push toward possessing their dream. This drive must be tempered by the knowledge that God is the co-creator in this process and He shows his 'goodness and mercy' to those who have a relationship with Him.

What power there is in the following verse – "The eyes of the Lord thy God are always upon you, from the beginning of the year even unto the end of the year."

It is empowering to know that God Almighty has His eyes upon you, an individual. With billions of people in this world, He has His eyes on you, not just one day, but all the time. With His eyes on you, watering your dream, how can you fail? This is an assurance that causes you to push forward, yet to rest in the fact that you have divine assistance. The final chapter in this book speaks clearly of what God will do.

It is this assurance that also keeps you from giving up, to persevere.

Every God-given, God-inspired dream is God-driven to its completion if we don't give up. Yes, you have to work hard. Yes, you have to overcome obstacles and setbacks. Yet there is a calm assurance that your dreams are on their way.

Now, only three months old, the Temple Baptist Church needed not only land, but also a place to meet. There was steady growth of the congregation and it was a challenge for Pastor to house 700 people every week. After meeting initially at Meharry Medical College, the church assembled in schools, under a tent (for revival) and settled temporarily in the Hillcrest Seventh Day Adventist Church, graciously opened by their leader, Elder Harold Kibble.

The people rallied and paid $56,000 for the first twenty-eight acres of land on Kings Lane. We were told by the land developer and owner that if we were late or missed a payment, that land would be repossessed. Needless to say, that did not happen, to the surprise of the developer. We know he was surprised because one of our members, Mother Ada Calloway, was his cook and housekeeper and overheard a business conversation.

The need now was to move forward and build. After months of unsuccessfully searching for an architect (remember that we were a fledging congregation with 'no track record'), Pastor called for a period of fasting and praying. The neighborhood prayer groups began to seek the Lord's guidance. There was no answer, only rejection after rejection. It was just when it seemed as though all hope was gone that an architect literally walked through the door of the room where Pastor and deacons were praying. He had heard from another Pastor that we were looking for an architect.

Look at God! He had His eyes on us. We were so grateful.

Let's review the steps:

You discover who you are and realize that God set a purpose for your life as expressed by this dream. What is your perception? What are your core beliefs and attitudes?

Assess your priorities – See where you are now.

Determine who you want to be and where you want to go.

Decide on appropriate actions – gather knowledge, choose team

Strategies – get help from team, overcome obstacles (external barriers) and opposition (internal barriers)

Work hard and connect to your relationship with God through Jesus Christ. You must possess passion.

Encourage yourself!

These projects and strategies need to be specific, measurable and have a date of completion.

For example: Your dream is to lose weight.

Dream: to lose weight

Specifics: to lose 50 pounds

Starting point and date: September 3 - weight 190 pounds

Ending point and date: December 3 - weight 140 pounds

Perception: When I lose this weight, I will fit the size 10 dress I just bought. I will feel much better. I will look better in my clothes. I will be able to walk up the stairs without getting winded. I will have more energy at the end of the day.

My **core belief and attitude**: I know that I can lose this weight by the desired date. God is my helper.

Purpose statement: I know that by losing this weight, I will be honoring my body, the temple and thus glorifying God. I will be better able to serve Him in a healthy body.

Partners to help: my sister, my personal trainer, my physician, YMCA

Possession: I am going to do it! My projects and strategies include a new eating plan, an exercise plan for each day, prayer and accountability provided by my trainer and sister. I will not be discouraged by ups and downs, realizing that this is all part of the process.

You then plan each day, with a 'to do' list.

According to the complexity of your dream, the process could involve months or even years of activities such as planning, projects, gathering resources, and recruiting partners. The purpose of this book is to inspire you to dream and understand the basic process.

So now, you are in the process of possession. The next step and principle is ***perseverance.***

Perseverance- Stay on the path

Don't give up!

> "When you get into a tight place and everything goes against you till it seems as though you could not hold on a minute longer, never give up then, for that is just the place that the tide will turn." **Harriet Beecher Stowe**

A mother of seven children, a wife, a woman whose mother died when she was four, this author knew what it was like to be at her wit's end. She supported the Underground Railroad, in the 1800s, and housed many runaway slaves. She received an education in a male environment and spoke out against slavery.

In 1850, when Congress passed the Fugitive Slave Law, prohibiting assistance to fugitives. Stowe was moved to present her objections on paper, and in June 1851, the first installment of **_Uncle Tom's Cabin_** appeared in the antislavery journal *National Era*. She had a dream of social justice and the end of slavery.

This 40-year-old mother started a national debate. Upon meeting Stowe, Abraham Lincoln allegedly remarked, "So you're the little lady who started this Great War!"[1] She was in a tight place many times.

There are times when we all get into those tight places. We get stressed and distressed. **We are at our wit's end.**

Have you ever heard the phrase: I'm at my wit's end? The word, **wit**, has several meanings. As a noun, it means the natural ability to perceive and understand. As a verb, it means to know. Synonyms for wit are: brainpower, sense, resourcefulness, competence, mind, sanity.

When you are **at your wit's end,** you can't make any sense of your situation. You are at the end of your resourcefulness. You have tried everything, and nothing works. You have thought your best thought. You have shot your best shot. You have done all that you know how to do. You are losing your mind, your sanity. You are distressed. This is a step beyond discouragement.

What about the word, stress?

Stress/distress – The word, distress in Latin means a narrow passage. It's trying to get through a tunnel that is not big enough. You've gone so far with your determination that you can't go up or down... and you can't go forward.

You're stuck.

Have you ever been there? Your dream is stuck and you are stressed out trying to find a way to get unstuck. When you are stressed out, you really do 'lose your mind." There is a physiological reaction that affects your brain cells and affects your ability to think. You are at your wit's end.

What do you do when you are at your wit's end?

Looking at Psalm 107, we see that it doesn't stop at the verse that says, "They reeled and staggered like drunken men and came to their wit's end." Psalm 107: 23-30 (ASV)

There's another verse, and in the verses that following, that speak clearly to us about what happens when you come to the place called "wit's end."

First of all, God brings us out of distress. This text is talking about businessmen, merchant marines who are well acquainted with the sea. They are going about their daily business of merchandising and trade and commerce.

But on this particular day, while going about their normal activities, a storm comes up on the sea.

The wind blows seemingly out of nowhere. High waves come and the ship is taken up by the waves. As the waves rise, the ship suddenly, as quickly as it rises, falls back down and the ship drops, seemingly into the depths of the sea. That's a distressing situation.

There are times in one's emotional, spiritual and professional life that one feels like that little ship on that storm-tossed sea. You have been going about your daily business, moving toward your desired haven (your dream) and then, out of nowhere, there comes a storm.

We realize that life is not lived with an absence of stress. The only people with no stress are six feet under. Stress can actually be motivating and helpful to a certain degree. So life is not always a matter of getting rid of stress, but learning how to cope with overwhelming, debilitating stress.

What did the psalmist do?
He cried out to the Lord...and the Lord brought him out of his distress.

Ultimately, God is the one who must rescue you.

When you are distressed, you are physically, emotionally and spiritually exhausted. You are anxious. You can't think your way out.

You must be still and allow God to work. He will bring you out of your distress. He works on you internally and emotionally.

He also calms the storm. He works on the outside.

Whether your storm is on your job, in your finances, in your love life, with your children, with your spouse, He can handle it .Sometimes the storm is just within you.

The psalmist says that God comes in such a way that he makes the storm a whisper. The final promise in this Psalm is that God will bring you to your desired haven. After you have struggled, and come to the place called your wit's end, and you have wrestled with the storm and you don't know what to do about it... God comes.

You're all torn up because of all the pressures that are all converging on you. He not only brings you out of all that, He also takes you where you want to be. That's a promise.

Ask for God's help. Your persistence depends on it.

Prayer:

Eternal God, our Father, we thank you that you speak to us through your word. Bless us as we seek your help with the storms of life –with the distresses of life that get us stuck on the way to our dream. Help us to trust you to bring us to our dream, our desired haven, where there is peace and joy, success and accomplishment. Amen!

> *"Achievement is not always success while reputed failure often is. It is honest endeavor, persistent effort to do the best possible under any and all circumstances."*
>
> Orison Swett Marden

Chapter Fifteen

Overcoming Opposition and Obstacles

When you develop persistence, you will face opposition.

> ... and this they were confident that they should effect. The hindering of good work is that which bad men aim at and promise themselves; but good work is God's work, and it shall prosper. (Read Nehemiah 4: 1,4-9 (TMSG)(Matthew Henry Commentary)

Good work is God's work.

Nehemiah was in the process of dreaming with his eyes wide open. It was a God-given dream that had God's eye and favor upon it. He then proceeded to speak the dream and form his dream team.

Nehemiah 4:17,18 (ASV)

When the Temple Church was built, my husband decided to build the gymnasium first so that there would be a multipurpose space. If the sanctuary had been built first, we would only have had just a 'preaching' room.

There were people in Nashville, critical of us for leaving such a comfortable situation and moving into a situation with a dream and no resources. **Our faith in God was the greatest resource and is also your greatest resource.**

With our God-given dream and God-given dream team of 256 people, we began to build. **People said it couldn't be done**. They said that we would fail. We were ridiculed in the very same way Nehemiah and his team were. We first needed land. God provided the opportunity to purchase 28 1/2 acres of land for a miraculous amount of $56,000.

Through the continuous sacrifice of this small group of hard-working people, God allowed us to possess and own the first acreage.

When my husband announced that we were going to build a $1.2 million dollar sanctuary, the critics really had a lot to say. Some critics came around just to see the project fail and became critics on the inside.

Our dream team, under my husband's leadership, continued to build, many times having to verbally defend the dream on their jobs, in the grocery store, on the city bus, even in their own congregation.

We know what it is like to experience opposition.

If you have not yet experienced opposition, keep on moving toward your dream. You will.

What do you do? What did we do? What did Nehemiah and his dream team do?

- **They prayed.** You've got to get up in the morning praying. You've got to go to work praying. You've got to pray before you go to sleep at night.

I'm not talking about these knee-bent, body-bowed prayers; but I'm talking about prayers in which you talk to your Father like you are His child and you say to the Father, "We've got a work to do and we cannot do this by ourselves. We need you to help us and we need doors to be opened. We need friends to be raised up and we need our finances blessed so that we can do more than we have ever done before."

- **Get prepared**. In the scripture we are studying, Nehemiah developed a **strange strategy**. He says to watch the enemy. Half of them worked and the other half watched. In other words, you must **do something to protect your dream.**

You should nurse your dreams and protect them through bad times and tough times to the sunshine and light which always come.

Woodrow Wilson (1856-1924)

As a dreamer, you must inform and inspire your dream team to **'tighten the ranks."** That means that they are aware of the opposition and with courage are ready to defend the dream. They must strap on their swords (the Word of God) and keep it close to them. Every now and then, draw your sword. Read it to yourself: "The Lord is my light and my salvation, whom shall I fear? The Lord is the strength of my life, of whom shall I be afraid? "(Psalm 27:1, 2 NKJV)

Prayer, preparedness and partnership. My husband told us that we all had to work together. In the Bible account, Nehemiah's team had a 'mind to work.' Nehemiah said they worked so hard they didn't even have time to take off their clothes. They worked morning, noon and night.

They didn't even stop for a drink of water. They were FOCUSED.

That's how you overcome opposition. Stay focused, don't give up, pray all the time, be creative, look for the 'high ground', assess the landscape for a better path, defend your dream with the word of God.

Nehemiah and his team built the wall. Rev. Michael Lee Graves and his team built the million dollar Temple Church building.

Through looking at the ocean while writing this book, I have become fascinated with surfers and their mindset. They face the obstacle of a four to six foot wave of water over and over. This wave, like any obstacle obstructs or hinders their progress as they see to go out into the ocean. It is from observing them that I gathered some lessons on how to deal with obstacles.

Surfers:
- Head into the obstacle. - When encountering an onrushing whitewater wave, go straight into it.
- See it as an opportunity, have no fear

- The bigger the wave, the more excited they become
- Study the nature of the wave- they take the energy of the wave and harness it to their advantage.
- Carefully choose the wave; they don't ride every wave- Wave judgment and timing are crucial to success. They know which wave to paddle for and which to let pass and the timing – when to start paddling, how fast, how much to arch their back, and when to get to their feet . They learn from experience. If they find that the waves are more powerful than they thought and they are not in total control of their surfboard, they do not try to go all the way out. They stay inside and work on their skills and get stronger for the next swell. It takes years of practice.
- Develop experience and skill through trial and error
- Fall and get up over and over.
- Surf with a partner- Partner gives moral support, keeps you up when you get frustrated, and helps with your timing.

There are many lessons on facing obstacles from watching surfers.

In the book of James, we find the same attitude toward obstacles, trials, temptations, tests and challenges. All of these are different but all can be obstacles.

Let's focus on how we can approach and deal with such:

[2]Consider it a sheer gift, friends, when tests and challenges come at you from all sides. [3]You know that under pressure, your faith-life is forced into the open and shows its true colors. [4]So don't try to get out of anything prematurely. Let it do its work so you become mature and well-developed, not deficient in any way.
[5]If you don't know what you're doing, pray to the Father. He loves to help. You'll get his help, and won't be condescended to when you ask for it. [6]Ask boldly, believingly, without a second thought. People who "worry their prayers" are like wind-whipped waves. [7]Don't think you're going to get anything from the Master that way, [8]adrift at sea, keeping all your options open.

James 1:2-8 (MSG)

The more familiar King James Version of verse 2 says:

[2]My "Brethren, count it all joy when ye fall into divers temptations."

We are to have JOY when we face obstacles? Why?

Look at Romans 5:3-5

"And not only that, but we also glory in tribulations, knowing that tribulation produces perseverance; and perseverance, character; and character, hope. Now hope does not disappoint, because the love of God has been poured out in our hearts by the Holy Spirit who was given to us." (NKJV)

[3]There's more to come: We continue to shout our praise even when we're hemmed in with troubles, because we know how troubles can develop passionate patience in us, [4]and how that patience in turn forges the tempered steel of virtue, keeping us alert for whatever God will do next. [5]In alert expectancy such as this, we're never left feeling shortchanged. Quite the contrary—we can't round up enough containers to hold everything

God generously pours into our lives through the Holy Spirit!

Romans 5:3-5 (MSG)

When we have obstacles, we develop patience. As we develop more patience we gain experience. As we develop more experience, we have more hope. In the process of dreaming with our eyes wide open, we need hope.

However, there will be tribulation. What is tribulation?

The Latin derivative refers to a device, a machine (tribulum) with rollers and plates that would roll across grain or grapes, producing with pressure either oil or wine. This device would, in circular motion, press over and over.

When obstacles come, it is not a pleasant experience. The scripture does not tell us that we are not hurt, or pressured, or squeezed. We are, and many times we put on a happy face believing that, if we don't, we are denying our faith in God. Not so. Feeling the pain of trial, tribulations, and obstacles makes us no less spiritual.

However, with the eyes of God, the perspective of God, we realize that, although we are not joyful now, that there will be good later. We believe that, as Psalm 30:5 says, "Weeping may endure for a night, but joy comes in the morning."

We can say with confidence, "This, too, shall pass."

So we develop patience.

This word**, patience**, does not mean a passive, unemotional sitting around and waiting for a change. It means to see things from God's perspective. God's perspective is that something good is going to come out of this. Patience means not giving up on your God-given dream. It means you are going to 'hang in there." It means that you are going to trust God even when it seems He has abandoned you.

This kind of perseverance comes first from knowing God, from a relationship with God. If that relationship is not one of knowing and **trusting**, you will have difficulty in having God's perspective on obstacles.

When you don't trust, things get difficult, stuck; you get anxious, stressed, at your wit's end. You begin to doubt your dream, your partners, and your ability to make your dream come true. You may compromise and in turn actually sabotage your dream.You are doing all you can do; now relax and let God do His work.

My youngest granddaughter, Michayla Leigh, loves to tell her older brother, who is very active, to "relax, enjoy your day." Many times, I must remind myself to do the same. Relaxing means that you trust God and God's timing.

One thing you learn from experience from falling over and over and getting up every time, is that **God is not in a hurry. What He is going to do, He will do in His own time**. We are in the age of "instant", "fast access", "fast food". God is not locked into time. So often what we must realize is that God sees the entire 'movie' while we are locked into a photograph of the present time. He knows the beginning, the middle and the end.

We like to sing the song, "Please be patient with me, God is not through with me yet…When God gets through with me, I shall come forth as pure gold".When we have experience and have been put to the test, we look forward to something good, like gold. We have hope.

What is hope? It is the expectation of good.

The hope, the expectation of good, is produced by the perseverance toward the dream God has given to us.

The process, not the dream NOW BECOMES THE IMPORTANT FOCUS.

Up to this point, we have focused on making the dream a reality. God wants to know that, whether you see your dream come true or not, you really have the response in hard times that He expects. That response is patience, perseverance and hope.

God rewards this proven character (James 1:12) with the crown of life. That is the ultimate dream. It doesn't matter what material dreams you may have accomplished; it doesn't matter what political or public fame you attain; it doesn't matter who you know.**What matters is that your God-given dream gives glory to God and that you receive the crown of life.**

Quotes to ponder:

Great spirits have always encountered violent opposition from mediocre minds.

Albert Einstein

"The ultimate measure of a man is not where he stands in moments of comfort and convenience, but where he stands at times of challenge and controversy."

Dr. Martin Luther King, Jr.

"History had demonstrated that the most notable winners usually encountered heart-breaking obstacles before they triumphed. They won because they refused to become discouraged by their defeats.

B.C. Forbes

"I have learned that success is to be mea-sured not so much by the position one has reached in life as by the obstacles he has overcome while trying to succeed.

Booker T. Washington

There's no thrill in easy sailing,
When the sky is clear and blue.
There's no joy in merely doing
Things which anyone can do.
But there is some fulfillment
That is mighty sweet to take,
When you reach a destination,
You thought you couldn't make.

Unknown

Chapter Sixteen

Climb out of the coffin

What do you do with dead dreams?

> [14]Wake up from your sleep,
> Climb out of your coffins;
> Christ will show you the light!
>
> Ephesians 5:14 (MSG)

"Harlem"
What happens to a dream deferred?
Does it dry up
like a raisin in the sun?
Or fester like a sore -
And then run?
Does it stink like rotten meat?
Or crust and sugar over -
like a syrupy sweet?

> Maybe it just sags
> like a heavy load.
> *Or does it explode?*
> - Langston Hughes, 1951

Lorraine Hansberry, the daughter of Carl and Nannie Hansberry, grew up in a successful black family where both of her parents were political activists campaigning against Jim Crow laws – the race based legislation that epitomized the era of segregation in America. She selected "Montage of a Dream Deferred" as the preface to her play, "A Raisin in the Sun."

This Langston Hughes' poem implies that segregation and racism played a major role in preventing African Americans from attaining the "American Dream."

What was his dream? He dreamt of a world where there is love and freedom for all. His world was not that dream. His dream was deferred. It had not yet happened.

What does happen to a dream deferred? Even worse, what happens to a dream that has died?

Most people are not living their dreams. They live their lives thinking, "I wish I had…" Maybe you can identify with this statement. You felt the call of God on your life and realized a specific purpose. Maybe you were called to be a teacher, a musician, an artist, a counselor. Maybe God's purpose in your life was to be a writer, a missionary, a nurse. Perhaps your dream was to succeed in business and to invest money to help spread the gospel throughout the world. Maybe you just wanted to stop just existing from day to day, but to be passionate about your life. You may have even possessed your dream and started working on reaching it.

What happened? Why did it die?

Some dreams die because the dreamer couldn't handle the pressure of obstacles- criticism, lack of finances, lack of encouragement, and lack of partners. Some of us think we have run out of time. There could be a thousand reasons. But as time passes, we look back on our lives and wonder what could have been. This situation is not limited to one age group. There are many young people who either have no dreams or have, at an early age, given up on their dreams. Their lives have taken a direction away from their original plan.

Ephesians 5:14 says, "Arise from the dead." The Message Bible is even more descriptive. It challenges us to **climb out of our coffins.**

Can you imagine being at a funeral and someone sits up and gets out of their coffin? After the initial shock, we would probably be very happy that our loved one was alive again.

Jesus was good at disrupting funerals and raising the dead. There was a man named Jairus. His little girl died, He came to Jesus for help. As soon as Jesus heard that the little girl was dead, he immediately told Jairus: "Do not be afraid; only BELIEVE." Jairus believed. His daughter was raised from the dead as Jesus leaned over her and spoke these words of life, "Little girl, I say to you arise."

Mary, the sister of Lazarus, was weeping. Jesus saw her and asked where Lazarus was buried. After weeping himself, he came to Lazarus' tomb. Lazarus was very dead – if there is such a thing! He had been dead for four days. Jesus said, "Did I not tell you that if you BELIEVED, you would see the glory of God? Jesus prayed to his Father and embalmed Lazarus walked out. (John 11:32)

Abraham and Sarah were old. Their bodies were old. God had promised that Abraham would be the 'father of many nations." Against all hope, Abraham BELIEVED and so became the father of many nations, just as it had been said to him. The dream seemed to have run out of time. The natural mind said: "You're too old. It's too late." **But God said otherwise.**

Look at Moses. He knew his purpose was to be Israel's deliverer, but he went 'ahead 'of God. He faced the criticism of his people. They asked, "Who made you ruler over us?" Moses ran away to the wilderness, got married and started taking care of sheep for forty years. God spoke through an angel in the burning bush and resurrected the original dream along with renewed energy.

Whether your dream never really lived, lived for a short time or has been dead for forty years, God challenges you today to tell your dream to climb out of the coffin and live. All you have to do is ask Jesus to help you and BELIEVE. Once your dream is revived, you go back to perception, purpose, possession, perseverance.

> ➢ *Benjamin Franklin was past 80 when he helped draft the U.S Constitution.*
> ➢ *Ghandi was in his 70s when he launched India's struggle for independence.*
> ➢ *Georgia O'Keefe, after becoming blind, learned pottery in her 90s.*
> ➢ *Grandma Moses started painting at 78 and kept going until she was 101.*

➤ *My mother, in her sixties, went back to college to complete her bachelor's degree, then her master's degree. She graduated from American University with her Ph.D. degree in philosophy, with honors. Dr. Berlene Byrd Newhouse achieved her life-long dream!*

Linda Michelet was 63 years old. She had dreams of singing. She offers advice for other women her age: "It's time to become fearless and do things they never thought they could or would, to come into their own."

Linda decided "to put my dream in my own hands and try to become a performer. It was terribly frightening to me. I think it's probably the most frightening thing I've ever done."

Peggy Lee had recently died. Linda grew up listening to Lee's records; she knew the lyrics and her styling. So Linda took a deep breath, approached Terry Currier, owner of Music Milennium, contacted a great group of musicians in Portland and began to sing. She has even recorded her CD, "Linda Lee Michelet Live." She dresses up in glamorous gowns and people love her. Linda feels she put her dreams off long enough to be amazed at her success. She is grateful that they've finally come true. She wants women of her age to know that it's not too late to revive those old, dead dreams and do it.

Chapter Seventeen

Wait for your dream

(From Sermon: "When morning is all night coming" -Pastor Michael Lee Graves)
                                     Habbakuk 1, 2:2-4

Night is a dark time – actually and figuratively. It is a time when it seems as though nothing is happening. **Night!**

- ✓ For Brenda Cooms, a homeless woman, living under a bridge, it was the night when her shoes were stolen.
- ✓ Linda Lee Michelet's night experience was when she divorced her husband at age 46 and sold all her furniture.

✓ For the Graves family, our "night" was those days when, for twelve years, the dream of a sanctuary was on "hold." We were struggling financially; people were tired of the struggle. About 300 people left the church for various reasons. It was night.

The darkest time of night is just before dawn. The most difficult time in the dreaming process is just before the dream becomes reality. It is often at this point that the stress is the greatest and one tends to give up.

This is no time to "throw in the towel." Your dream may be on life support, but it is still alive.

It is hard to believe that morning is coming, but it is. In my husband's sermon, "When Morning Is All Night Coming," he speaks of this night experience. The night can mean experiences such as sickness, family problems, deferred dreams or the economic crisis of purchasing expensive braces for your child or a car breakdown. Everything is in disarray. One thing after another pops up and it seems as if morning is all night coming.

We must wait on our dream.

All seems to be on hold. We get upset with God when we have to wait on our dream. We often challenge and question God. When we question God, we get an answer. He says:

1. **Write the vision,** let others see it – make it plain, simple.
2. **Wait for it to come**. It is coming. The answer may not come in the first month, the first year or several years, but it will come.
3. **Wait with eager anticipation**, not worry. It's sort of like waiting for ketchup to come out of the bottle. You know it will come. You must live by faith.

In waiting, one day can make a big difference.

(From sermon, "What a difference a day makes." Luke 23, 1-12 – Pastor Michael Lee Graves)

If we can only make it through the seemingly endless night, day is coming. It was night for the people who saw Jesus' body placed in Joseph's tomb. (Luke 23, 24: 1-12) He had just been crucified. The women that loved Jesus were sad, depressed and hopeless. It was a dark and difficult time when their dream of a new life with this great leader had been dashed. Their dream, they thought, died on the cross. It was Friday night and then Saturday.

It is now Sunday morning, very early. They are wondering what they would do when they arrived at the burial site. They were going to prepare Jesus' body with spices. How would they move the stone that covered the opening of the tomb so that they could enter?

When they arrived, not only was the problem solved (stone removed), but also the most wonderful and incredible thing happens - the tomb is empty. At first, they are puzzled. Then out of nowhere it seemed two men, light cascading over them, stood there. The men said, 'Why are you looking for the living One in a cemetery? He is not here, but raised up. Remember how he told you when you were still back in Galilee that he had to be handed over to sinners, be killed on a cross, and in three days rise up?' Then they remembered those words." Luke 24:1-7 (MSG)

The dream was still alive.

What a difference between Saturday and Sunday!

God has a way of surprising us. What a difference a day can make. One day we are down, disheartened, depressed. The next day, we find new life, hope and dissipation of our disappointment. If we can persevere, just one day can make a difference between failure and success. God gives a glimpse of glory and success after your darkest moments.

You realize with just one glimpse that God is still working and you can keep moving toward your dream. The good news from the grave is this: **what seems to be dead is alive.** Dreams that seemed dead yesterday can be alive today with God's power of resurrection.

As a volunteer at a local 'crisis' center for pregnant women, my goal was to get that frantic, often hopeless woman to give her situation at least one more day before deciding to abort. Many times, after one day the obstacles seemed a little less intimidating, less dramatic, and more manageable.

There was a popular song, "What a Difference a Day Makes." The lyrics celebrate the fact that " twenty-four little hours ... the sun and the flowers where there used to be rain." One day makes a difference. Maybe that day is really a week, a month, or perhaps even a year. The important thing is to wait. Persevere.

Don't give up on your dream yet. Give it one more day.

Principle Six

Positive Spirit-Be positive

I t looks as though your dream will never come true. You are really trying to hang in there and give it one more day. Something just isn't right. You are beginning to doubt yourself, your purpose, your partners, your dream and maybe even your God.

Doubt is most often the source of our powerlessness.

So what can you do? This sixth principle should perhaps be in the first section of the book because it is so fundamental. This is the principle of a positive spirit. A positive spirit gives you the power, the ability and might to move past doubt which is created by fear.

A positive spirit is the consistent ability to see the good and the God in everything and everyone. How do you get it?

Chapter Eighteen

Have an "I Can Do Spirit" and look up

In our Christian school, Temple Academy, all of the students, principal and teachers memorized Scripture verses. Every week of the school year, a new verse was introduced, explained and then memorized.

The first verse of the school year was always Phil. 4:13 – "I can do all things through Christ who strengthens me." Even the youngest students, some of them four years old, grasped the concept of this verse. To reinforce the internalization of these powerful words, they made an "I" can. These were simple, empty coffee cans on which they placed the letter, "I". Whenever they said, "I can't", the teacher or parent would ask: Where is your "I" can. They would then quote scripture as they remembered the decorated coffee can.

My daughter, Ayanna, who was a student of Temple Academy, took her "I" can to sit on her desk in college and relates the number of times this can reminded her of this simple yet profound verse.

There is power in the way you think. Open your mind and begin to think positively. You will then begin to speak positively and live with a positive spirit.

> ➢ A **positive spirit** prevents you from quitting when it seems as though your dream is unattainable.
> ➢ A **positive spirit** allows you to make adjustments necessary to go over, around or through hindering situations.
> ➢ A **positive spirit** provides you the power to see life through Romans 8:28 "lenses". These lenses frame all things good and bad, happy and sad, up or down, forward or backward, on target or detoured. It says, "All things work together for good for those who love the Lord and are called according to His purposes."

You must believe that no matter what you're facing now, you can do all things through Christ.

Stir it up! – You've got the power.

There is power in the way you think. Maybe you need to focus on changing what my husband would call your 'stinking thinking."

"You block your dream when you allow your fear to grow bigger than your faith." Mary Manin Morrissey

Changing your mind involves intentionally moving past fear, loving your dream again, filling your mind with hope and a positive spirit. Joan quote

How do we do this when we live in a basically negative world?

Norman Vincent Peale, the father of Positive Thinking says, "Practice hope, as hopefulness becomes a habit, you can achieve a permanently happy spirit."

Realize that you have all the 'ingredients" you need to do this. You have **perception, purpose, possession and perseverance**. These are all gifts from God placed in you.

Now stir it up!

It's like placing potatoes, carrots, meat and seasoning in a crock pot. You will get a great stew, but you must stir it up. **Stirring it up means that you actively and deliberately move past fear**. When you keep your eyes on Jesus, you will soon lose sight of your fears.

It also means that you take the focus from yourself.

There is the story of a little girl who had on her bedroom wall a picture of Jesus above her head. On the opposite wall, she had a mirror. When she sat up in bed, she could see herself in the mirror, but she blocked the image of Jesus. However, when she moved herself out of the way, she could see Jesus in the mirror. So it is with us. Realize that this dream is God –given and as you stir up the gift of God within you, take your eyes off of yourself and place your focus on Jesus, you can keep moving forward.

You must not only keep your eyes on Jesus, but also look up.

The Israelites were taking a detour around the land of Edom. The people became irritable and cross as they traveled. They spoke out against God and Moses. "Why did you drag us out of

Egypt to die in this godforsaken country? No decent food, no water – we can't stomach this stuff any longer. "So God sent poisonous snakes among the people, they bit them and many in Israel died. The people came to Moses and said, "We sinned when we spoke out against God and you. Pray to God; ask him to take these snakes from us." Moses prayed for the people.

God said to Moses. "Make a snake and put it on a flagpole. Whoever is bitten and looks at it will live." So Moses made a snake of fiery copper and put it on top of a flagpole. Anyone bitten by a snake who then looked at the copper snake lived. (Numbers 21:4-9)

The power of looking up.

There are times when our dreams are in pro-cess, God is blessing us and we take matters into our own hands. We lose sight of the fact that we need God and we speak against the Lord and his power in our lives.

We become so familiar with the blessing of God, especially when God is faithful day after day. We take for granted the blessing of God. We must be careful of despising the blessing of God. Be grateful for what you have.

Be careful of what you say.
Be careful of how you think.
Realize God's protection and guidance that has brought you this far in the dream process.

When you are on the verge of your dream, there will be trials and trouble. The tendency is to blame God. God isn't going to move these trials. Some things you just have to live with and some things you have to walk through and some things you just have to journey on anyhow.

God will fix the situation.

Resist the temptation of putting God in a box. We want God to do what we want Him to do, when we want Him to do it. God doesn't always act the way we want Him to act. God has not removed the stuff that hurt you, but He has promised the remedy. The remedy is in the upward look.

This is simple. Look up – develop a positive spirit. Trust that God will bless you and keep your dreams alive.

God said, "I'll bless you, but you've got to look up." Stop looking down feeling sorry for yourself, wanting everybody to feel sorry for you. You will have a pity party all by yourself.

A few ways to "Look Up"

1. Pray/ Read positive scriptures.

Write positive affirmations from scripture. Place in strategic places in your home.

2. Breathe –

Take your mind off the situation by noticing your breathing. Relax.

3. Laugh

When you feel blue, immerse yourself in the humor and go for a stomach-aching full laugh. Deep laughter improves your immune system and helps you keep life's problems in perspective.

4. Return to Nature

Go for a walk in a park, sit by a fountain, or gaze at a poster of your favorite ocean or mountain scene. Reflecting on a beautiful natural scene can lift your spirits.

5. Make a gratitude journal

Make a brief list of three to five things or people in your life for which you are grateful. Reflect and identify the positive way they impact your life.

6. Get out and help someone

Send an uplifting e-mail. Call an elderly relative or friend. Offer a few minutes of your time to baby-sit or walk the dog for a busy neighbor. Helping another moves your focus and will improve your spirits.

7. Exercise

A brisk walk or any other form of physical exercise will improve your mood. The physical activity will help lift your mood.

8. Apologize

Guilt and regret can hang around us like a lead weight, bringing on mild depression without our awareness of the cause. Pray and ask God to reveal people you need to ask for forgiveness. After apology, leave the past.

9. Listen to music –

Whatever music is calming to you, turn it on and relax.

Principle Seven

Power Beyond Yourself

Chapter Nineteen

God is your greatest partner

He cares about you and your dream.

In the dreaming process, make sure that God is on your team. When God is on your team, you have a quiet comfort, confidence and power beyond yourself.

What we know about God and what we do for God have a way of getting broken apart in our lives. When we know that God has given us a dream (**dream seed**) and we were born for the purpose of glorifying Him, we realize that He is our **greatest partner.**

Here you are, standing on the verge of your dream becoming reality. You have done all YOU can do.

So- what's next to do?

Give your dream to your greatest partner, God.

Let **God take over.**

After all, He is the one who...

...gave you the dream (**perception**)

...gave you life (**a purpose**),

...sent you people to help (**partnership**)

... allowed you to (**possess**) the dream

... gave you the strength to (**persevere**)

...and remain (**positive**) in the process.

When you give your dream to God, what will God do?

He provides comfort, confidence and power. How?

1. **God will shelter you.** When trouble comes, there is no need to go running and trying to find shelter. You must live in His presence. Our security is in God. Trust Him. He will rescue you from every trap and protect you from deadly things and hide you with his feathers. He is faithful.
   God will protect you. In a day of terrorism, we can become paralyzed by fear and immobilized in our quest to make our dreams come true. We must rely on God's protection. Sidney and Saundra moved ahead on the day we will all remember, September 11. God does not give us fear, but power, love and a sound mind. (I Timothy 1:7)
2. **God will lift you.** When you are down, He will do what you cannot do on your own – lift your head. There are times when you are so weakened – physically and spiritually, that the only thing you can do is pray. He will encourage you. Look up to Him.
3. **God sends His angels when you pray.**

4. **God will make you the victor**. It is only God who gives you power over lions and snakes. He helps you to persevere. He guides you through unknown territory as He did Abraham. . He will keep those negative situations and people from killing your dream.

5. **He will answer when we call on Him**. Trouble will come but He has promised to be with us in trouble. (Based on Psalm 91)

6. **God will, if we "commission" Him, take our dream beyond our wildest imagination. He gives you power (ability to get things done) beyond yourself.**

"Now to Him who is able to do above and beyond all that we ask or *think* – according to the *power* that works in you - …"

Ephesians 3:20 (HCSB)

Paul in this powerful passage from his letter to the church at Ephesus knew that the purpose of his life work was to glorify God. In his feelings of inadequacy, he is surprised and sees it as a gift that God is handling the details of his move from dream to reality. This passage in Ephesians is a prayer for spiritual power – **a power beyond our abilities that we can access.**

"God can do anything, you know – far more than you could ever imagine or guess or request in your wildest dreams?"
Ephesians 3:20 (MSG)

God takes your dreams to another level. When He does, you get a glimpse of glory, the true meaning of your purpose in life – not money or success in man's terms – but success in God's terms - to glorify God and become more like Jesus Christ. When you realize that you did not do it, you give glory to God, who is **the power beyond yourself.**

I thank God for His great power!! Without Him, nothing would be possible. With Him, all things are possible!!

I have lived to see many of my dreams come true. I know the process well! Perception, purpose, partnership, possession, perseverance, positive spirit and power beyond yourself are principles that guide me daily. Surely, God has transformed our "dream seed" into reality. I walk into the manifestation of that dream every Sunday. I thank God for a church where people love God and each other, where there is 'ministry that matters', a church that functions not only on Sunday, but throughout the week, meeting the needs of the people of the church and the community - the fellowship now known as "The

Temple Church" in Nashville, Tennessee. It is beyond our 'wildest dream.'

No money has become several million dollars. No building and no land has become a six building campus in five locations and over 100 acres.

Two people have become over 4,000 people who minister to the Nashville community, Haiti and Belize

God can and will do more than you could ever dream.

As you have read this book, I pray that God has **opened your eyes.** On the day I submitted this work to the publisher, my morning meditation from Oswald Chamber's , *My Utmost for His Highest* , was entitled: **What's next to do?** How appropriate!

I share with you his suggestion:

"Put everything in your life afloat upon God, going out to sea on the great swelling tide of His purpose, and your eyes will be opened."

My prayer for you as you **dream with your eyes wide open** is expressed by Paul:

"I ask Him to strengthen you by His Spirit... that Christ will live in you as you open the door and invite Him in. And I ask Him that with both feet planted firmly on love, you'll be able to take in with all Christians the extravagant dimensions of Christ's love...Live full lives, live in the fullness of God."

I invite you to pray:

Dear God, I know that You have called me for a special mission. Every Christian has a mission for Your kingdom. I know you have given me a dream. I see it with my eyes wide open. I pray that every day I will seek and follow Your guidance, allowing You to work through me to accomplish your purpose. Help me to persevere. If my mission is to feed the hungry, take care of my family, reach out to the hurting, work with a group of children, preach to the multitudes, lead a nation – however big or small – I want to pursue it and bring glory to You. Thank you for finding me worthy of ministering through. In the name of Jesus. Amen

Live your dream! Glory to God!!!

History of the Temple Church, Nashville, Tennessee

The Temple Church was founded August 8, 1977 at the American Baptist Theological Seminary in Nashville, Tennessee. The first Temple worship service was held on August 7, 1977 at the Kresege Learning Resource Center on the campus of the Meharry Medical College. Sunday services were held at the rented facilities of the Hillcrest Seventh Day Adventist Church until January 4, 1980 when Temple entered its present facility at 3810 Kings Lane.

Under the able leadership of the Reverend Dr. Michael Lee Graves, Temple made great strides in the growth of its membership and programs to serve the needs of the community. It began with the original two, Michael and Eleanor Graves, and now has a membership of over four thousand. The growth of Temple's membership and its over fifty-three ministries owes its success to God and its 256 founding members who wanted to establish a church that would make a difference in the Nashville community.

The gymnasium, fellowship hall, chapel, day care center, commercial kitchen, library and the office suites were built initially. This was done because Pastor Graves believed that if the entire complex could not be built at once, these areas would better serve the membership and the community. Thus, we completed Phase One of the building program.

In 1991, we began construction on Phase Two, which included a sanctuary, baptismal pool, choir loft and bell tower. Thanks to God, we moved into our new addition on September 13, 1992. The Temple Church now sits on 100 acres.

In August of 2004, Bishop Michael Lee Graves, sensing the urgency of the moment, publicly named his assistant and mentee, Darrell A. Drumwright as his successor. After Bishop Graves transitioned home to be with the Lord on December 7, 2004, Pastor Drumwright assumed the office of Senior Pastor on Sunday December 12, 2004. Under his leadership, the church has continued to grow and has become debt free in a recessionary time. He continues the lead in the spirit of excellence and commitment to a balanced ministry. Pastor Drumwright is a wonderful, well-educated, spirit-filled leader who loves his people. We love him. Temple Church believes "The Best Is Yet to Come."

CPSIA information can be obtained at www.ICGtesting.com
Printed in the USA
BVOW010827100812

297510BV00001B/2/P